From
Strength

From Strength to Strength

Daily meditations in Lent

D.W. CLEVERLEY FORD

MOWBRAY
LONDON & OXFORD

Copyright © D.W. Cleverley Ford 1987

First published 1987
by A.R. Mowbray & Co. Ltd,
Saint Thomas House, Becket Street,
Oxford, OX1 1SJ

Typeset by Oxford Publishing Services, Oxford
Printed in Great Britain by Cox and Wyman Ltd., Reading

British Library Cataloguing in Publication Data

Ford, D.W. Cleverley
From strength to strength: daily meditations
in Lent.
1. Lent—Meditations
I. Title
242'.34 BV85

ISBN 0–264–67084–1

From strength to strength go on,
Wrestle and fight and pray;
Tread all the powers of darkness down,
And win the well-fought day.
(C. Wesley)

They will go from strength to strength:
Psalm 84.7 (BCP)

ACKNOWLEDGEMENTS

I would like to express my appreciation of the contribution made to this book by my wife who has read a page of the typescript each day in order to check the level for the ordinary Christian reader for whom the book is intended. Also Miss Barbara Hodge of Canterbury for typing and sometimes re-typing my handwritten MS; and the Diocesan Secretary at Canterbury for providing facilities for this work.

Lingfield 1986   DWCF

Introduction

This is a book for ordinary lay Christians who wish to use the season of Lent for some extra spiritual exercise. But being busy people with only limited time and opportunity it needs to be short, straightforward and related to the world in which we live.

The main part of the book consists of a series of daily meditations on one aspect of human life seen in its relation to the divine life, pinpointed with a biblical text and concluded as often as not with a prayer. Each week of Lent has been given an overall theme, and the meditations have been grouped accordingly. The meditations begin on the Monday before Ash Wednesday, making the first week preparatory, and end on the Saturday in Easter Week with the theme 'our sources of strength'.

There will be some with sufficient background who will wish to consider the themes in rather more depth than daily meditations in the rush of life make possible. In an attempt to meet this a short commentary is added at the conclusion of each of the weeks exploring the theme of the week with greater fulness and sublety. The wise reader will think it best to leave the tackling of these commentaries to the greater leisure of the weekends.

In addition some questions have been provided which may prove useful for discussion groups.

The aim of Lent is to make those who observe the season spiritually stronger. If this book helps to that end it will not have been written in vain.

DWCF

Contents

Salvation in practice

O come, let us sing unto the Lord:
let us heartily rejoice in the strength of our salvation.

Psalm 95.1 (BCP)

A train not a roundabout

Hebrews 13,14 (NEB) '. . . we are seekers after the city
which is to come.'

This is Monday. For many people it means back to
the old grind after the welcome break of the weekend. Monday appears to come round so quickly.
There always seems to be more grind than break. No
wonder the question nags, Are we getting anywhere?
Is life nothing but a never-ending merry-go-round
with very little 'merry' in it? We go to work to earn
the money to buy the food to make us strong to go to
work to earn the money . . . The feeling is well-
known. No wonder depression sometimes takes
over. No wonder brash attempts get made to kick
over the traces. Boredom is a curse.

A quick answer to the problem is to organize more
parties, more excitements, perhaps more occasions
for 'letting down the hair'. And the man or woman is
stupid who does not plan to surmount the dullness of
routine with excursions of one kind or another.
Otherwise life is only existence. Even so there has to
be a deeper answer, something less superficial, and
in the end more satisfying. It is wrapped up in the
belief that our lives are not really comparable to a
merry-go-round at a fair-ground although sometimes
this is how they feel. No, they are like a train. They
are going somewhere. We are all on a journey to a
destination, and what we do on the way counts,

however apparently trivial. So what I do today or don't do, what I skimp or perfect matters. When this belief is held, life begins to make sense. We begin to experience salvation in practice. We are making for a destination like a train. It is not a roundabout. To strengthen this belief is one of the purposes of Lent. What we believe conditions how we react not only to Mondays but to everyday of the week.

Thought for the day
  One the object of our journey,
  One the faith which never tires,
  One the earnest looking forward,
  One the hope our God inspires:
      (B S Ingemann, Tr. S Baring-Gould)

TUESDAY BEFORE ASH WEDNESDAY

Makeshift Salvation

Acts 27,44 (NEB) '. . . some on planks, some on parts of the ship. And thus it was that all came safely to land.

When a ship breaks up in the violence of a storm at sea, the crew, passengers and all have to abandon it and make for land *as best they can*. The struggle for safety is a desperate, makeshift business. So it was with Paul's ship on the voyage to Rome wrecked off the island of Malta. There was nothing for it but to jump overboard and get to the shore somehow,

3

which thing everyone did. So 'some on planks, some on parts of the ship . . . came safely to land.'

This is a picture of the human side of the salvation which God offers us. It is not the only picture of salvation given in the book of the Acts of the Apostles but it has this distinctive feature that salvation is shown as a desperate makeshift business for us in our experience of it. There are many facets to this comprehensive word 'salvation' as used in the Bible but here the main idea is rescue or deliverance. Those on board were in danger if they stayed there. Their only hope of safety was to cast themselves into the sea, grab what they could and somehow propel themselves to the beach. No chance to be choosey here. No chance to be intellectually superior or socially superior. Anything that would float would serve, any piece of wood.

The Christian experience of salvation may, often does, operate like this. It is a desperate makeshift affair. A remembered fragment of a hymn, half a prayer-book collect, a snippet of crude theology, some saintly individual (perhaps not even saintly), an overheard remark, a fundamentalist revival address, a pilgrimage to some holy shrine – anything about God which seems to float, we grab it and somehow manage to reach a haven of peace in our desperate struggle. Never despise the bits and pieces by which you came to know God for yourself. Do not despise them when you have reached the shore of a well-rounded evangelical/catholic/reformed faith in which you give due place to reason. It does not matter how

4

you came ashore so long as you did. Salvation is a process which begins rough.

Prayer
>Thank you, Lord,
>for the spiritual plank
>I managed to grasp,
>saving my soul.
>Guide me now
>to firm land.

ASH WEDNESDAY

The effort required

1 Corinthians 9.25 Every man that striveth for the mastery is temperate in all things.

We have all heard of a Marathon, the twenty-six mile race that attracts thousands of runners and millions of spectators. Similarly in St Paul's day, everybody in Corinth would be familiar with athletic contests. Easily therefore the Apostle could compare our earthly life with a race. We are all running towards a destiny beyond this life. We are not running around in circles.

Granted that for a few professionals in our Marathons the aim is to break a time record, but for most contestants it is to finish the course and not drop out. This is where the analogy fits in the race of life. There are ostentatious drop-outs motivated by protest against society. They are a minority. Over against them are the private and secret drop-outs. They simply drift through life taking what comes and grumbling at it. Their number is very great. Then there are the physical drop-outs, that is the men and women who no longer bother about their shape or appearance. And last, but by no means least, the spiritual drop-outs, that is those who used to live by standards and principles but have now abandoned the effort.

This word *effort* is the key. To stay in a race without effort is impossible. Salvation in practice also requires it. And effort in turn means discipline. And discipline means temperance in all things. It means strength to say 'no'; strength to say 'no' to indulgence in drink, food, time wasting and empty frivolity. For the tiny minority of workaholics it means temperance in that sphere too. If we can't say 'no' to anything we have lost our freedom, in which case we desperately need Lent, for that is the time set apart for winning back personal mastery, as well as going from strength to strength. What we may have to give up is a private matter, but not to be willing is to risk becoming a drop-out of some kind, and that is serious. It may mean jeopardizing our salvation.

Thought for the day
    We cannot be strong unless we are temperate.

THURSDAY

What is wrong?

Romans 3.23 (NEB) For all alike have sinned.

We had better face the truth head on – we are all sinners. All other doctrines of the Christian religion are faith concepts but not this one, not the doctrine of original sin. We only need to look around to see that sinfulness is a universal characteristic of human nature. And we ourselves are not the exception.

Maybe we try to excuse ourselves. Original sin is the hangover from our evolution from lower forms of life. Possibly; anyway as regards our animal instincts. This does not however erase the sorry sight it offers in the human story since the world began.

Perhaps we attempt to slough off a sense of guilt by reflecting that we are not individually responsible, we are caught in the network of our relationship to the human family. Bad blood in one parts affects us all.

Even so there are personal and individual sins. We did treat that employee unfairly. We did not give our employer the benefit of the doubt. We did lead that man/girl 'up the garden path'. And in addition to these transgressions, implying the breaking of accepted rules of behaviour, there are failures to live up to our own best intentions. We have fallen short of even the standards we have set for ourselves. Laziness could be the reason.

So wriggle this way and that as we may, the diagnosis of our condition by St Paul is sound – 'For all alike have sinned'. Maybe those recent voices which tell us we need not in consequence grovel have a point, but we had better own up. We are sinners. Salvation in practice begins here, and unless we do begin here we shall get nowhere in the progress towards spiritual strength. We must face facts.

Prayer

> 'Holiness I've none to plead,
> Sinfulness is all I see,
> I can only bring my need;
> God be merciful to me.'

(J S B Monsell)

FRIDAY

Saved for Service

Luke 5.10 (NEB) 'Do not be afraid,' said Jesus to Simon; 'from now on you will be catching men.'

No one would have thought so. All night long Simon had failed to catch a single fish. There he was by the Lake of Galilee washing the futile nets, a veritable chore on account of their emptiness, futility scored all across his clouded face. What heart could he find to attach himself to the ever growing circle of hearers on the shore close by, fascinated by the words of this freshly-come preacher from Nazareth – Jesus.

But the preacher commandeered *his* boat. He used it as a kind of pulpit preaching to the serried ranks of listeners on the shore. Simon had to listen then. He couldn't help it. But what overturned his sullenness was not the sermon but its sequel. He was bidden pull out into deep water and to start fishing. What madness! But Simon's protest froze on his lips. Soon there were fish everywhere, in the nets, in the boat, under the feet . . . .

Simon felt beaten. 'Go, Lord, leave me sinner that I am.' He felt he had come to the end of himself. After all his boat was the place where he did his work, earned his living and prided himself on his skill. It was there that he was a failure, and it was there that this Jesus, entering it, was a resounding success. But a spiritual law was at work. We must needs feel our weakness before we can receive Christ's strength.

Jesus did not however leave Simon. He saw potentiality there. 'Do not be afraid' he said 'from now on you will be catching men.' And so it worked out. In due time Simon (called Peter) was catching men *with his preaching*.

To be saved from our sins, and the repetition of them, is a start. When however Christ is welcomed into our everyday life (our boat) we are saved from futile labour to accomplish beneficial service for our fellows. This is salvation in practice.

Prayer

'Take my life, and let it be consecrated, Lord, to thee:'

(Frances R Havergal)

9

Salvaging chores

Zechariah 4.10 (NEB) Who has despised the day of
small things?

This is Saturday. Many people catch up with chores
on Saturdays. They have to. Most of us take a poor
view of chores but we cannot escape them altogether
even though our modern gadgets have eliminated
much of the drudgery. After all the lawn will not
mow itself.

Chores can however be a blessing. Take an extreme
case but not so extreme it has nothing in general to
say. In the early days of that most hurting experience
– bereavement – there are a hundred and one (as we
say) routine jobs to be tackled forthwith. This is a
mercy. When the spirit is low, near to breaking point,
if the truth were told, what is required is not a
thrilling, demanding, exciting experience, but a dull
plodding labour. Anything else could only inflame
the wounds still more.

Perhaps we need to change our minds about our
chores. If we hate them, resent them and grumble
about them, they will do us harm spiritually. Suppose however we recognize a potential in our chores.
Suppose we could see them as providing a period
when the mind and spirit can almost 'go a blank'.
After all it is not only the body that needs a rest, so
does the soul. Chores can be therapeutic. They can
save us from being pressurized by providing a little

space where our hands and feet must receive almost all our attention.

We even need a rest from the spiritual. There is imminent danger in trying always to speed along in top gear. The religiously inclined need to beware. So our chores could contribute to our salvation if we recognize that one of the meanings of salvation in the New Testament is wholeness, or wholesomeness. We might almost say balance.

Prayer
> 'The task thy wisdom hath assigned
> O let me cheerfully fulfil;
> In all my works thy presence find,
> And prove thy good and perfect will.'
>
> *(C Wesley)*

SUMMARY FOR THE WEEK

Salvation

Salvation has become a word with a distinct and almost exclusive religious flavour. Maybe we fight shy of it. It suggests a form of sentimental piety. This is unfortunate, narrowing down what is actually very broad. As it happens we cannot do without the word 'salvation'. Anyone who tries to live the Christian way must be a disciple or learner of the Christian vocabulary, and one of the basic words is 'salvation'. There are others like 'grace', 'faith', 'justification' and

'reconciliation'. Lent could be a time for 'rubbing up'
our Christian word list.

Salvation as presented in the Bible is not to be
restricted to the atmosphere or tactics of a religious
revivalist meeting. It covers the whole of life, physical
as well as spiritual, corporate as well as individual.
Salvation has to do with wholeness. Basically the
meaning is deliverance, deliverance from whatever
may be acting as a check on the wholeness, healthi-
ness, fullness and enjoyment of life, in the community and in the personal life of individuals.

In the Bible salvation is sometimes deliverance from a
national foe such as the Egyptians or Philistines. At
other times the enemy is plague, illness, bondage
(such as the exile in Babylon) or death. In the New
Testament salvation is basically restoration to health
and rescue from danger. Thus we read of Jesus
saving or curing (NEB) a woman with a haemorrhage
(Mark 5.34), and a man smitten with blindness (Mark
10.52). Salvation in these cases is something visible
and tangible. He also saves, rescues, his disciples
from a storm, and Peter from drowning. In all these
cases Jesus is the Saviour. There is no hard and fast
distinction between saving someone physically and
saving someone spiritually. Men and women are
seen as wholes in the New Testament not as two
separate parts – body and soul – somehow stuck
together. So when someone is threatened either
physically or spiritually the whole is affected and
salvation is the requisite. Not surprisingly then Jesus
used the same words to the woman suffering her

physical infirmity as to the woman deeply conscious of her sins 'Your faith has saved you.' (See Mark 5.34, Luke 7.49). There was an occasion when Jesus showed that he could save as well in one area of life as in another (Mark 2.1–12). Salvation stretches right 'across the board'.

We see then how salvation refers to the present, but it also refers to the future. Theologians would say it has an eschatological reference, that is to say it looks to the end-time or consummation of the age (Matthew 24.13). We need to be saved *for* God's coming kingdom in the future. We need to be saved *from* the wrath of God, from condemnation, perdition and from final death.

In every connexion of salvation in the Bible, God is He who does the saving not man himself. Salvation is never conceived of in terms of man pulling himself up over a period of time by means of a process of education, religious or otherwise. There is always a break, almost a revolution. God has done something for our salvation which alters the whole of life, its past, its present and its future. We may come slowly to grasp what has been done. There may be no dramatic conversion. The truth may gradually dawn on us, but dawn i⁺ must. We do not make the sunrise – we *have been* saved.

The fact that we have been saved does not however mean that we need do nothing about it. God's action for us and in us is not automatic Our cooperation is required. To use theological terms – faith and works are not mutually exclusive. There are two aspects of salvation. On the one hand what God in Christ did and still does, calling for our faith; and on the other hand what we must do in response. So St Paul wrote in his letter to the Philippians (2.12,13) 'You must work out your own salvation in fear and trembling; for it is God who works in you, inspiring both the will and the deed, for his own chosen purpose.'

Let us summarize. By means of God's action in the life, death and resurrection of Christ we have been rescued, delivered and begun to be made whole; so we *have been* saved. Secondly, we can look forward confidently to the future and to the judgement of God beyond this life. Christ is our assurance. We *shall be saved*. Thirdly, we are *being saved*, being made more wholesome as we learn of Christ and follow his way, which in practice means self-giving for others' welfare.

It is possible to lose what we have. Lent operates as a warning and an opportunity. We can make our salvation safe. We can proceed from strength to strength by prayer and discipline.

2. THE FIRST WEEK IN LENT

Recognizing grace

The Lord shall give strength unto his people:
the Lord shall give his people the blessing of peace.

Psalm 29.10 (BCP)

Summoned by bells

Psalm 95.6 (BCP) O come, let us worship

Sunday, since the dawn of the Christian era, has been the day for worship, and for centuries Christians have been summoned to it by bells. Worship is the Church's first duty, it even takes priority over service to the community, the poor and the needy, imperative though that service is. This is because worship is the Church's witness to the way in which the wholesomeness of life is safeguarded. If we forget who is the real God or set up some substitute of our own making, human relationships weaken, even to breaking point.

Worship is a corporate activity. Not only do we join with other worshippers living now, because we meet in a place where worship has taken place before us, and because we use prayers and hymns our forefathers have used, we unite ourselves with the Church down the ages. Worship cancels out individualism and isolation. When we enter a place of worship to worship we belong. We belong whether or not some other worshipper shakes our hand. Belonging makes for wholesomeness, isolation for faith-debility.

We are summoned to worship. That we are summoned by bells shows that worship is not meant to be a doleful, but an enjoyable experience. We are going forth to meet a God who comes forth to meet us. He

16

starts before we think of coming to him. Theologians call this *Prevenient Grace* – God favouring us, who are unworthy, with his outstretched arms of welcome. All this, and much more, is rooted in God's coming to our world in human form – Jesus of Nazareth.

The Sunday summons
> 'O worship the Lord in the beauty of holiness!
> Bow down before him, his glory proclaim;
> With gold of obedience, and incense of lowliness,
> Kneel and adore him: the Lord is his name.'
>
> (J S B Monsell)

MONDAY

The divine circumstance

Psalm 139.2 (BCP) Thou art about my path, and about my bed:

During Lent some extra spiritual exercise may be attempted, even reading this book could constitute such. Nevertheless the days of Lent cannot be very different from all the other days of the year for most people. There will be the same train to catch, the same family to be fed, the same shopping to be done, the same all absorbing problems in business. Lent will have to take a back seat.

Come to think of it, that God, the God who brought the world into being and sustains it moment by moment, and ourselves as part of it – that He, God, and the things concerning him, should have to take a back seat, is *odd*. Not odd perhaps for the godless, but odd for us who acknowledge and worship him. But wait! Have we really relegated God to the margin of our daily lives simply because we cannot be thinking of him all day long?

Take the case of the happily married man or woman. (The analogy fits equally well with a close friend). Are they thinking of each other all day long? Yet is it not true that their busy and absorbed life succeeds the more because it is played out against the tacitly accepted background of the spouse's, or friend's, love and concern? The truth is, the private background sustains the public foreground. If the background cracks, so does the foreground. Do not broken marriages tell this story?

So let us, on this Monday, understand how God is *the great circumstance* of our lives. God is the one who is *standing around* us all the time whether we are aware of him or not. Hear the words of Psalm 139 again, 'Thou are about my path, (conscious life) and about my bed:' (unconscious life). God's presence does not depend on our effort but on his grace. It is what he freely provides.

A confession
      'Jesus, these eyes have never seen
      That radiant form of thine;
      The veil of sense hangs dark between
      Thy blessèd face and mine.

I see thee not, I hear thee not,
Yet art thou oft with me;
And earth hath ne'er so dear a spot
As where I meet with thee.'

(R Palmer)

TUESDAY

But for the grace of God

Ephesians 2.5 (NEB) 'It is by his grace you are saved'

When in the face of the downfall of some man or
some woman caught and convicted of some serious
moral breakdown, perhaps quite unexpected, the
comment is made – 'there but for the grace of God go
I' – the motive is not to be lightly dismissed. The
phrase touches on the reality of the human predica-
ment and the reality of the divine provision.

'There but for the grace of God go I'. Who can tell if
he/she were faced with the alluring temptations that
other person faced he/she would not fall in precisely
the same fashion, and with the same consequences?
The ruin of a promising public career can come with
one sudden unpremeditated lapse. The woman
caught him when he was off his guard and tired with
unremitting toil. The man played up to her loneliness
till she could hold out no longer. Which of us can
boast that we should have done better *given those
circumstances?* The wise person will identify with the
petition in the Lord's Prayer, 'Lead us not into

19

temptation'. We cannot be sure that we should come out unscathed. Therefore we shall be slow to condemn.

Our human weakness is not all that lies behind this telling phrase 'There but for the grace of God go I'. There is also the grace of God. How many times unknown to us have we been saved from falling due to no merit on our part whatsoever? This is what grace is – God's free favour to the undeserving. For no reason we can fathom, God steering us away from some situation in which we should probably have 'come a cropper'. And if now we are in good standing we shall be wise not to blow our own trumpet. God has been steering us round awkward corners and along precipitous paths of which we were oblivious.

To think over
> Slow to condemn but quick to acknowledge divine grace.
> This is the Christian way.

WEDNESDAY

Out of the blue

2 Samuel 1.26 (NEB) 'Your love for me was wonderful'

If at any time there has come into our lives some good man or some good woman whom we admire, we should count the fact as evidence that the grace of God is upon us. It is people that lift us up, not possessions, position or fame. In so far as the story of the human race is one of progress, outstanding individuals are the cause of it.

One of the experiences of sheer grace is a successful marriage, that is a marriage when the constant love of both partners contributes to the individual stature of each. Neither the man, nor the woman, went out to find that spouse, the contact came 'out of the blue'. Call it romantic by all means, for so it is, but the grace of God lies behind it, and no other reaction is appropriate but humble thanksgiving. And of course to break what is God-given is unthinkable. One does not fly in the face of grace.

But marriage is not the only sphere where the grace of God operates in the provision of good persons who attract us. There are friends, male and female. We should be faithful to friends. One or two may have joined us early on as we were stepping out on the road of life and have since died. Someone else may have come with us to a parting of our ways after which contact was all but impossible. We should not forget that in his providence God sometimes provides us with the friends we need for a specific period of time only. They were the right friends for that time. There are others who join up with us for the latter stages of life's pilgrimage and 'keep right on to the end of the road'. The message to us is always the same – see the good people whom we love and who love us and who have come to us 'out of the blue' as evidence of God's concern for our welfare, and remain loyal to them and to their memory.

Prayer

> Lord, I thank you for . . . ., for . . . .
> and for . . . . .
> Keep me loyal to those you have sent
> to accompany me on the road of life,
> for it is of your grace that they have come.

THURSDAY

Providence and responsibility

Deuteronomy 8.10 Thou shalt bless the Lord thy God
for the good land which he hath
given thee.

That some people are more richly endowed than
others by nature and by personal effort is a fact of life.
Possessions however, not even riches, are inherently
evil. When God called the children of Israel out of
Egypt it was not to settle them in a desert but in a
good land, a land more productive than their neighbours', a land so good it was said to be 'flowing with
milk and honey'. But they were to husband it well,
and they were to see to it that none lacked the
necessities of life. Rich people there would be in
God's promised land but they were not to crush the
poor to make themselves rich, and certainly not to
crush them to make themselves more rich.

Riches and possessions carry with them responsibili-
ties. It is not having money but what we do with our
money is the test. This being so, the rich actually

occupy 'a hot seat' in the community. They live with their judgement over their heads. For this is the peril of possessions. They blind people. They make them insensitive to the plight of others. The result is little people, little in personal stature, little in compassion whom God will judge, and whom also their neighbours without possessions will judge.

Providence is one of the great mysteries of life. One man is called to plenty, another is called to suffering. We cannot tell why. What is required is that we accept as somehow within the providence of God the place in which we find ourselves and *live responsibly there*.

Prayer
> Lord, you have brought me to this place;
> I did not choose it.
> It is better than the place which some occupy;
> it is worse than others.
> I do not know why this should be my lot,
> but I will try to live responsibly in it,
> believing in your providence,
> and relying on your grace.

FRIDAY

Peace of mind

John 14.27 My peace I give unto you.

There can surely be no question but that one of the most widespread human needs at the present time is for peace of mind. No doubt it has always been so but in the modern world, on account of the widespread news coverage of the world's calamities the battering of the soul is intense. The television screen and the sound radio call for our compulsive attention, but if they enlighten they hurt as much. For people living alone they can become destructive of every vestige of tranquility.

In addition there are personal worries. Those mortgage payments which have to be met. The possibility of 'redundancy'. Adolescents drifting into unsatisfactory attitudes. The compelling and disturbing attraction of 'the other man', 'the other woman'. The list is long.

Some wrongs are straightforward though strained. For such, peace of mind is possible through confession, owning up, apology – call it what you will. God's forgiveness is readily available. The load is lifted. Other problems cannot so easily go away because they are environmental.

There are people who seek a sort of peace by artificial means; drink, drugs and furious activity; but they only deaden pain, they do not face the problem. Others by an act of will retreat into a private world – 'What goes on round the corner is none of my business'. The method works to some extent provided the will is sufficiently strong to sustain it, but as often as not with a bad conscience thrown in. It is a retreat from the battle.

It is doubtful if peace of mind can be *achieved* altogether, but it can be *received*. Peace of mind comes when we let go, not into the hands of fate but into the hands of grace, God's grace, the God who loves us, going before us and following us all the way. Those willing to believe this – and the word 'willing' here implies effort – will receive peace of mind *as a gift*. 'My peace I give unto you' said Jesus, 'believe in God, believe also in me.'

Prayer
    Into thy hands, O Lord, I commend my spirit.

SATURDAY

Playing at religion

Matthew 23.13 But woe unto you, scribes and Pharisees, hypocrites!

These words could be spat out with biting sarcasm and scorn. Hostile critics of the Church echo them with vituperative language against an organisation they hate. But did Jesus hate anyone? Did he hate the scribes and Pharisees? Is not the New English Bible a more sensitive rendering at this point? – 'Alas for you, lawyers and Pharisees, hypocrites'. What we encounter here is Jesus's sigh over these outwardly, and in a way, well-meaning, religious men. 'O the pity of it' he is saying in effect 'You go to enormous lengths with your religious practices, so diligent, so public, but you come nowhere near the reality of religion. You are playing at it. You are like actors on a stage. You put on a splendid show; but when the play is over in public what are you behind closed doors?'.

The Church needs to take this warning to heart, including bishops, priests, deacons and lay members. We can put on a good show. The English have a genius for ceremonial. The trouble with all shows is that they breed pride on the part of the performers. And when it comes to religion, humble dependence on the grace of God is nowhere to be seen.

What the Church finds hardest of all is to *live* by God's grace. Start out we may, with a clear recognition of that grace in having called us to salvation, but after a time we reckon we are earning our salvation. Even receiving the sacrament of God's grace in the Eucharist becomes a meritorious work. And haven't we observed Lent? After all the man/woman next door hasn't bothered! So don't we deserve credit? The truth is, till we come round to see, and never cease seeing, that all is of God's grace, we are only playing at religion, we have missed the real thing.

Prayer

> Lord, the Church has nothing it did not first receive.
> Help me to see my faith too in this light,
> lest I become a hypocrite.

SUMMARY FOR THE WEEK

The doctrine of grace

If there is one doctrine which can be said to bind the Old and the New Testaments together, it must be the doctrine of grace. This doctrine declares that our salvation stems from God's loving kindness (Hebrew, Chesed) and not from our human worth; which, by the way, does not mean that man is worthless. The story which the Bible has to tell (and the Bible presents its doctrines in story form), is all of a piece from beginning to end. God chose to be his people those who in themselves were unworthy of his love. Salvation is a favour bestowed. It is of grace (Greek, Charis). It is never a reward earned.

Grace however can be misunderstood. It can be thought of in mechanical terms as if it were a kind of power like electricity. What we should need in this case would be to know which are the switches which control it. There has been a view that the Church is in possession of the switchboard. This will not do. Grace does not operate mechanically. Grace is more like the influence of a person. Think of it this way: Here is a school teacher confronting a new class for the first time. He looks at his pupils and they look at him – greatly wondering. What is life going to be like with these children? What is life going to be like with this teacher? The teacher knows that no progress will be made at all, the children will learn nothing from him, unless he *first* and *foremost* wins them. He, the teacher, must take the first step. He must take it even though the children in front of him look unpromising, and may be a bundle of problems. But being a wise and able teacher, he does win them; and in so far as they respond to him are they able to receive from him what he is competent to offer by way of instruction and learning.

Grace is like the personal influence of such a teacher. To be effective he has to take the first step in commending himself to his pupils. So God took the first step for Israel by bringing his people out of the bondage of Egypt. So Paul wrote to the Romans (Chapter 5.8) 'God commendeth his own love towards us, in that, while we were yet sinners, Christ died for us'. Theologians call this 'prevenient grace', the grace that goes before, or takes the first step. But it can be resisted. Grace is never automatic in its operation. It does not force. It does not override. It cannot because it is not that kind of power. On the other hand it can be received. It can be met with a response. The pupils in the class learn from their teacher when they are open to him, when they trust him, and especially so if they even love him. Another word for this kind of response is faith. So now we are in a position to make a theological statement drawn from experience.

We receive the grace of God by means of faith. St Paul put this down in black and white in his letter to the Ephesian Christians (Chapter 2.8) 'By grace have ye been saved through faith; . . . it is the gift of God.'

Once we have grasped how the power of grace is personal and not mechanical we shall not be asking why, if God is a God of grace, all are not thereby the recipients of his grace. To be effective grace, being personal, needs response. It is possible to withhold that response.

What are the means of grace? or to phrase the question another way. What are the channels by which the grace of God comes to us inviting our response of faith? Not surprisingly, since grace is personal, the person of Jesus Christ. He is the means of grace *par excellence*. There is also the Word of God ministered through the Bible with preaching and teaching. There are also the sacraments especially the Eucharist which is more than a memorial; it is a means of receiving Christ himself in faith. The world of nature too is a means of grace, available before as well as after the coming of Christ, as the non-Christian religions testify. But response there must always be. Grace to be effective must be met with faith.

3. THE SECOND WEEK IN LENT

Exercising faith

Seek the Lord and his strength:
seek his face evermore.
Psalm 105.4 (BCP)

The household of faith

Psalm 84.2 (BCP) My soul hath a desire and longing
to enter into the courts of the Lord:

To note what someone longs for is to discover where
he or she belongs. A Frenchman exiled for years who
has adopted the language and life-style of the country
where he lives is nevertheless a true Frenchman, a
Frenchman at heart, if he longs to see Paris again
before he dies. Longing is an indication of belonging.
So the composer of Psalm 84, cut off from the Temple
worship at Jerusalem, shows himself a true son of
Israel although living in a foreign land. He longed for
the household of his people's faith.

There is something doubtful about someone's Christian profession if all longing for participation in
Christian worship is absent. It would be proper to
enquire if he really belonged. It is also a serious
spiritual condition when prolonged and avoidable
absence from Church ceases to worry. The Christian's Church is the Christian' home. It is the
household of faith (Galatians 6.10). It is the place to
assemble, where the men and women of faith meet. It
may be a very ordinary home, even an unsatisfactory
home, but it is still home and any Christian who
ceases to care about it has partly died inside; it may
mean his/her faith has died.

One of the terrible consequences of World War 2 was
the thousands of families driven from their homes in

Eastern Europe by the advance of the Russian armies into Eastern Germany. They fled west carrying only meagre handfuls of possessions. Those who settled down most quickly and successfully in their new lands were those who found the local Church there. It seemed like a piece of the old home and it served as a bridge by which they were able to build a new life in a new place.

It is a rough test of the reality of our Christian profession to ask ourselves how much Church attendance means to us. It is a rough test of whether a local Church is fulfilling its function, or not, to enquire how far it is a home for the local community. It has been observed that in English village life where the Church is not the centre of the community how weak is the community in comparison with those places where the opposite is the case.

Prayer
> Bless, O Lord, my local Church
> and the ministry of clergy and people.
> Suffer me never to fall into the error
> > of despising it,
> > neglecting it,
> > or counting it of no importance
> for the life of our community.

The beginning of faith

2 Timothy 1.5 (NEB) I am reminded of the sincerity of
your faith, a faith which was alive
in Lois your grandmother and
Eunice your mother before you,
and which, I am confident, lives
in you also.

It is a mistake to imagine that Christian faith consists
first of all in swallowing, as it were, perhaps with the
eyes closed, tablets of doctrine. It is also a mistake to
reckon that the Creeds recited in Church have to be
accepted 'lock, stock and barrel' before the confession
'Christian' is allowable. Not that Creeds are unimpor-
tant. We must however understand what they are
for. They are guide lines for the life of faith. They say
in effect, 'Look this is what the Christian Church after
two or three hundred years of experience, knocked
this way and that in a hostile world, came to see was
the bed rock of what it believed. If it did not keep
close to these statements there was a real danger that
the faith would be whittled away altogether.

No, we do not, we did not come to Christian belief in
the first place through the gate of intellectual assent
to a set of theological statements, but more likely
because we loved our mother and she was a
Christian; or we were inspired by some teacher or
preacher whose personality drew us, or we felt
strangely warmed in finding ourselves in a Christian

fellowship, be it Church, club or school. Experiences like this cause us to wake up to a Spirit beyond ourselves. Such is the beginning of faith. It begins in experience.

In a recent book called *This time next week* the author Leslie Thomas lets us see into a typical boy's mind. It is a circus of excitements, full of heroes and villains, deeds and misdeeds. He dreams of scoring goals in football and capturing adoring girls. He does not see things in the way they are. Stones are for throwing, wood is for carving one's name on, trees are to be climbed. Such was *his* boy's mind till one day he suddenly found himself looking with wonder at cloud formation, at the shadows on still water, and how music is something more than to be whistled as loudly as possible through the teeth. He even began writing down what he wished to remember. He had woken up to beauty beyond himself *and was responding to it*.

Something like this is how we *begin* the life of faith. Call it conversion if you like providing you do not insist that it has to be dramatic or sudden.

To think over
    Love is the soil in which faith grows.

TUESDAY

Where proofs do not operate

Acts 17.27 (NEB) In him (God) we live and move,
in him we exist;

Here is a pair of 'teenagers' involved in a furious row; all because one is 'sold on' pop music and the other is a devotee of classical music. Each was endeavouring to prove that his brand of music was superior. But proof in this area is impossible. Art, unlike science, operates *chacun à son goût*, each one to his taste.

It is futile therefore to escort a man insensitive to great painting into an art gallery with the object of trying to *prove* to him that a Rembrandt on one of its walls is a masterpiece. All he can see is a funny old man, not worth the trouble of painting.

The truth is there are departments of life where proofs simply do not operate; and it cannot be asserted that therefore they are beneath consideration. Here is a scientist working at a laboratory bench impressive with complicated instruments. He is married. Did he choose his wife on a scientific basis? Did he weigh her, measure her, analyse her component parts? Did he even classify her? What attracted them to each other? Certainly nothing to do with the scientific method. Science doesn't operate in love. Is love therefore of no consequence? The answer is obvious.

So we must not dismiss religion because we cannot *prove* the existence of God. The truth is we cannot stand outside God and examine him scientifically because 'in him we live and move, in him we exist'. After all you can't examine your spectacles if you are wearing them, and you can't see without them.

To think over
> Faith does not operate with proofs but it is not unreasonable.

WEDNESDAY

Faith as decision

John 12.11 (NEB) . . . many Jews were going over to Jesus and putting their faith in him.

Here we have a clear example of faith as decision. We can picture the situation. People crowded round Jesus to listen to him. They had never heard preaching like it – so direct, so authoritative, and yet so winning. And then the works of healing! Who else could accomplish such? Not that everyone was convinced. The chief priests were dead set against him, resolved even to kill him. And so on the part of all who encountered Jesus there was much weighing up in the mind to be done. Which was the right line to take? To be for him? or against him? A decision had to be made. This is the point to grasp. Those who went over to him, those who decided for him became *in so doing*, people of faith. So we can know what Christian faith at bottom is – it is *deciding for* Christ.

This kind of decision is no rarity. Every five years at least in Britain we have to come to a decision which parliamentary candidate to elect. We listen to them, watch them and weigh up their policies. There is no 'cast iron' certainty that the party we choose will be able to fulfil what is promised. So our decision is an act of faith. It cannot be more than this, for it may, or may not, be well grounded.

There is however a big difference between these two decisions. The political decision may indeed turn us into a Tory, Socialist or an SDP member, and we shall take on the general attitude of the party as a result. The decision for Christ however is on a different scale altogether. It puts us into union with the living God in Christ as a result of which we become Christ-men, Christ-women with life of a distinctive quality. This distinctive life is called 'eternal life' and it is a present possession, not simply a future possibility. St John's gospel puts the matter with the utmost clarity, 'He who puts his faith in the Son' (that is decides for Christ) 'has hold of eternal life' (John 3.36). What could be more simple? but what more profound?

Prayer

Lord Jesus Christ:
I have gone over to you,
I have put my faith in you
receiving through it your eternal life.
Suffer me not to fall away.

THURSDAY

Little faith

Matthew 8.26 Why are ye fearful, O ye of little faith?

The lake of Galilee is singularly attractive in its setting. Nevertheless it was here that the faith of the twelve disciples of Christ all but foundered. They had great expectations of Jesus of Nazareth. But he seemed to let them down. At least that is what they thought. They were crossing the lake by boat as darkness was beginning to fall. The journey wouldn't take long but a heavy squall came on. This can happen on this lake. Then the water gets really rough and the wind fearsome. These twelve men were terrified. Their boat was being swamped. And all the time the One they looked to as Lord over all the perils of life (had he not dispelled long-standing diseases?) lay fast asleep on a cushion in the stern.

Didn't he care? They awoke him to charge him with callousness. They could hardly have been more wrong. But we all do it. When the storms of life break over our boat – illness, domestic troubles, accidents, failures, bereavement – in so far as we think about God at all we reckon we are on our own. God couldn't care less. No doubt these men, like ourselves, could wax lyrical over that lake in the stillness of some placid morning with the sun beginning to light up the sparkling water. 'Surely the Lord is in this place!' Of course he is. But he is no less there when it is torn with storms. This is what we forget. This is where the littleness of our faith shows

39

up. It shows up when fear gets the better of us and
we start making charges against God which cannot be
justified. Of course God cares. What is more, because
at the times of our calamities he seems to be inactive
(asleep in the stern) he has not lost control. And there
is this further point to notice about this story from St
Mark's gospel. Because the faith of these men was so
little, their intelligence was little too. After all was it
likely that the Lord having chosen, called and begun
to train these twelve men for the future would have
them all drowned together in a little boat on a little
lake in a little storm?

To meditate on
> God is love: and he enfoldeth
> all the world in one embrace;
> With the unfailing grasp he holdeth
> every child of every race.
> And when human hearts are breaking
> under sorrow's iron rod,
> Then we find that self same aching
> deep within the heart of God.
>> *(Timothy Rees 1874–1939)*

FRIDAY

Great faith

Matthew 15.28 O woman, great is thy faith:

It really was something that this woman had her faith
commended, and actually identified as 'great' by no

less an One than the Lord himself. And she an outsider. Not even a Church goer! She couldn't be. Not that she was an isolated case of commendation on account of faith. There was that Captain in the Roman Army of occupation (Matthew 8.5–10), an unloved body of men if ever there was one. He too was an outsider. Even Jesus was surprised by him. but you never know. This soldier was not the last one to be a man of faith.

But why was this woman's faith great? What was special about it? To start with – because she couldn't physically bring her demented daughter into Jesus's presence for healing. She had to leave the child at home. But she reckoned that distance did not cut off this healer from the exercise of his powers. (What a contrast with the twelve disciples who doubted their Lord's care although close to them in their boat but separated from them by sleep). She also reckoned that he being a Jew and she being a Canaanite made no difference. Racial difference would not affect either his compassion or his power. And thirdly, she was not 'put off' because he did not immediately respond to her request. So sure was she *of him* (that is the point), she persisted with her plea on behalf of her daughter. Therefore Jesus labelled her faith 'great'.

What was the outcome? A child completely recovered. And the lesson? Not that faith will see the possessor of it rewarded with everything he/she wishes; but faith which *sets no limits* to the Lord's love and power is that which will see extraordinary results. Little faith is that which does not master fear (yesterday's meditation). Great faith is that which is prepared to risk committing our deepest concerns to a *limitless* Divine compassion.

Faith is the human instrument by which the astonishing power of a compassionate God is set free *in this world*.

Prayer
> O help us, through the prayer of faith
> More firmly to believe;
> For still the more the servant hath
> The more shall be receive.

> *(H H Milman).*

SATURDAY

There are answers

1 Corinthians 13.12 (NEB) Now we see only puzzling reflections in a mirror, but then we shall see face to face.

One of the conclusions to which we must come sooner or later is that we shall not receive the answers to all life's questions. There are personal problems; Why did that young couple have to face a cot death? And philosophical problems; How can you say we have freewill when our parentage and our early environment were both determined for us conditioning what we are? And theological problems; How can you explain why if God is a beneficent creator, the history of mankind is almost one long story of suffering? People without questions must be people incapable of thinking, or maybe they refuse to think because it is too unnerving. They could even be people who fancy that faith removes the puzzles, which simply is not true. We have to learn to live with some questions without ever receiving answers.

Every now and again we encounter some man or woman, so irritated by the complacency of those with an unenquiring simple faith that he/she magnifies the problems making puzzles where there might be solutions. Perhaps such a person derives satisfaction from seeming to appear intellectually superior. This is poor. Not that the questions must be suppressed altogether; and for this reason, that when they are, the outcome is a falsely based assurance which may manifest itself as an unattractive religious smugness. No, we can have a solid faith, and one of the firm planks in it is that *there are answers* to our questions, and *one day we shall know what they are*. Or, as St Paul put it, 'Now we see only puzzling reflections in a mirror, but then we shall see face to face.'

Prayer

> Lord, grant me to know
> what I can know;
> and what is beyond me to know
> help me to believe
> that one day I shall receive the answer,
> through Jesus Christ our Lord.

43

The nature of faith

Faith is not a subject about which a Christian can justifiably have nothing to say. The word 'faith', or its equivalent 'to believe', occurs on almost every page of the New Testament. Faith is basic. The first description of the members of the Church in the Acts of the Apostles is that they *'believed'*. (Acts 2.44).

Faith however is not necessarily a religious word. A man may have faith in the United Nations, in Einstein's Theory of Relativity or some patent medicine. To a considerable extent we all have to live by faith. We cannot do anything else. In November 1985 there appeared in the newspapers what looked uncommonly like a splodge of white paint on a black surface. The caption underneath said it was a photograph of Halley's comet! Was it? What else could most of us do but believe it?

In the matter of faith everything depends on the object of faith. There is very little value in someone confessing he has faith unless he makes clear what he has faith *in*. It could be the 'man in the moon', or his lucky star, or an amulet he wears every time he boards an aircraft. In these cases his faith is equivalent to superstition. So the quality of faith – we might almost say the criterion of whether what is professed is faith at all – depends on the reasonableness or unreasonableness of what is believed *in*. Faith and Reason therefore are not wholly independent of each other as is sometimes wrongly supposed. They do

44

not belong to different worlds. A man is not unreasonable because he has faith, and faith cannot properly exist unless it has a reasonable object.

In the New Testament faith is almost always faith *in* and not faith *about*. So it has the meaning of trust. Moreover the object of faith is a person, namely Jesus Christ. This being so we must expect to be given an adequate presentation of his life, work, teaching, death and resurrection. Without it faith would be impossible. There would be nothing to trust. But having been presented with it we are called to decide for him. This decision is Christian faith. It involves our thinking and feeling and willing. It is a trusting response of the whole personality to the 'showing forth' of Christ.

We have to be careful lest we understand our Christian faith as the outcome or reward of our intelligence or perspicacity. This is not so. There is a warning against this faulty assessment in St Paul's letter to the Ephesians (2.8) 'For by grace have ye been saved through faith; and that not of yourselves: it is the gift of God'; or, as the New English Bible renders it 'For it is by his grace you are saved, through trusting him; it is not your own doing. It is God's gift, not a reward for work done.'

When Christ is presented to us his grace *enables* us to believe. We may refuse, but the enabling power is there *in the presentation*, whether it be in the preaching of the Word of God or in the ministry of the sacrament of the body and blood of Christ. These presentations, showings forth or proclamations are more than symbols designed to kindle the imagination. They are means of grace evoking faith. All this is why Christians cannot boast of their faith. They are not unusual persons possessed of some particular spiritual faculty to be compared perhaps with aesthetic appreciation which some can claim and others cannot. Faith in Christ is God's gift to all who will receive it.

But what does faith accomplish? Does it sharpen our wits? Possibly. Does it increase our sensitivity to unseen spiritual reality? Possibly. What however it supremely does, according to the New Testament is to *unite us with Christ*. This is faith's great work. So, according to St Paul, he who believes is dead with Christ (Colossians 3.3), is buried with him (Romans 6.4), is raised with him (Colossians 2.12), lives with him (Romans 6.8), is to be glorified with him (Romans 8.17), and will reign with him (1 Corinthians 4.8). Religious rules and regulations cannot possibly accomplish this, but faith is able. We cannot be Christians without faith, faith which unites to Christ.

A willingness for obedience

I will love thee, O Lord, my strength;

Psalm 18.1 (BCP)

Our duty of hearing

Romans 10.17 So then faith cometh by hearing, and
hearing by the word of God.

An Englishman once took a German friend to
Evensong in the chapel of one of the Oxford Colleges.
Knowing from experience of the choral tradition
there he took him proudly. And when the service
was over – both men transfixed by the beauty of it –
the Englishman could not help saying, 'Wasn't that
marvellous?'. 'Yes', replied the German, but with
marked hesitation, 'Yes, the music was wonderful,
and the worship sincere and uplifting, but it wasn't a
proper service'. His friend was disappointed. Surely,
he thought, he is not going to raise the well-worn
criticism that the congregation could not join in the
singing. But this was not the German's complaint. He
was too well-educated in his own country's great
choral tradition to complain of an aesthetic act of
worship. What he said was, 'It wasn't a proper
service because the word of God was not broken.'

The German would have been right had he been able
to complain that the word of God had not been read
aloud in the service for the worshippers to hear. A
proper service (to use his phrase) must give a place
not only for thanksgiving, not only for interceding,
but also for hearing the word of the Lord. The
German wanted more; he wanted the word 'broken',
that is, expounded as well as read. He wanted this

48

because without it worshippers might only hear words and not *The Word*. But a sermon is not necessary at every service provided that the word of the Lord is read, and that the reader understands what he is reading, and makes meaning 'come over' by the way he reads it.

This is the lesson. Christians have a duty not only to 'render thanks' and to pray but also to hear. They are required from time to time to hear the word of the Lord read aloud in the context of congregational worship. Christ is present when two or three are gathered together in his name, and he is the Word of God. Christians hear him when they hear his word read in the Christian assembly. And the Christian ministry has a special duty in this regard. It is to see that the Scriptures are so read in the worship that those who hear can't help listening.

Unless we hear we shall not have anything to believe.

An appeal
> Hark, my soul, it is the Lord;
> 'tis thy Saviour, hear his word;
> Jesus speaks, and speaks to thee,
> 'Say, poor sinner, lov'st thou me?
> > *(William Cowper)*

Christian action

1 Samuel 15.22 (RSV) Has the Lord as great delight in burnt offerings and sacrifices, as in obeying the voice of the Lord? Behold, to obey is better than sacrifice, and to hearken than the fat of rams.

There are some verses where the message is so plain, so straightforward, that neither careful study of the context, nor a modern translation, is necessary to see what it is. 1 Samuel 15.22 is one such. Obedience, that is, listening to God and doing what he says, is more acceptable to God than ritual worship (which does not mean that worship can be discarded).

What is it that God calls us to do? There is another verse which answers this verse with equal clarity – Micah 6.8, 'He has showed you, O man, what is good; and what does the Lord require of you but to do justice, and to love kindness, and to walk humbly with your God?'.

Doing justice in and for the community is required of Christians. It is the point at which obedience is called for; but not only there, it is required in the home and in the place of work. Husbands must consider their wives, and wives must consider their husbands. Children must be treated fairly by parents, and parents must receive what is their due from children. Employers must not exploit their employees, and

employees must not cheat their employers. Read
what St Paul has to say on this in Ephesians Chapters
5 and 6. No one is 'let off the hook'.

Church attendance, pious exercises, even the observ-
ance of Lent, do not make up for shabby human
relationships. Christian action is demanded of every
Christian. What do I believe? is a proper question,
but not more important than to be asked – What do I
actually do in consequence of what I believe?

Prayer
> How shall our life fulfil
> God's law so hard and high?
> Let Christ endue our will
> with grace to fortify.
>> Then justly
>> In mercy
>> We'll humbly walk with God.

(Albert F Bayley)

TUESDAY

Dead faith

James 2.14–17 (NEB) My brothers, what use is it for a
man to say he has faith when he
does nothing to show it? Can that
faith save him? Suppose a
brother or sister is in rags with
not enough food for the day, and
one of you says, 'Good luck to

you, keep yourselves warm, and
have plenty to eat', but does
nothing to supply their bodily
needs, what is the good of that?
So with faith; if it does not lead to
action, it is in itself a lifeless
thing.

Time and time again the Biblical truth has been
stressed in these Lenten meditations that our salvation, our wholeness – and this includes the health of
the community – cannot be achieved by human effort
alone. We certainly cannot run up a credit balance
with God in the matter of good conduct on the
strength of which he is bound to reward us with
eternal bliss. Faith in Christ is the way of salvation.
But the truth must also be set down in black and
white that unless there is something *to show for our
faith*, something in the way of good works (to use a
theological phrase), unless our faith leads to action, it
is dead; and nothing is more useless, nothing more
dangerous, than a dead faith. It leads to spiritual
gangrene.

It is the responsibility of government so to order the
affairs of the nation that its life is able to flourish in
peace and prosperity with opportunities for everyone
to develop his/her potentiality. This requires attention to welfare, order and defence. The Church
cannot sit loose to these necessities. Deprivation, bad
housing, poor job opportunities and decaying city
centres fall within the Church's concern so far as they
affect people. It cannot however, if it is to be true to

its calling, have social welfare as its priority, let alone the sum total of its activity. Its responsibility is the soul of the nation. People are not saved, they are not made whole, by improved social conditions alone. They may even be made worse. There must be something uplifting in which to believe. So the Church must proclaim its faith in season and out of season *and at the same time* show that its faith is alive by engaging in, and encouraging practical action to relieve necessity wherever it is found – and all because it cares about people. This is a sphere for Christian obedience. We dare not escape it.

Prayer

> Lord, should an opportunity
> come my way this day
> to relieve distress in whatever form,
> suffer me not to pass by
> on the other side.

WEDNESDAY

Reconciliation first

Matthew 5.23 (NEB) If, when you are bringing your gift to the altar, you should suddenly remember that your brother has a grievance against you, leave your gift where it is before the altar. First go and make your peace with your brother, and only then come back and offer your gift.

This sounds like a direct command on the lips of Our Lord calling for obedience, and so it is, but it is awkward! How awkward becomes obvious as soon as we transpose it to a contemporary setting. Here is a man on the way to Church. It could be Parish Communion, Cathedral Mattins or Evening Worship at the local chapel. Suddenly he remembers that one of his workmates is nursing a grievance against him. It has something to do with leave that had to be cancelled owing to pressure of work. What is he to do? Cut Church for today? Get on the telephone at once with the sole purpose of making peace with the offended man? But suppose he was due to sing in the choir! or to ring the bells! Suppose he was the minister due to lead the worship! People do bear grudges against clergy. Must there be no Eucharist that day, no sermon? not anyway till peace has been re-established.

Put in this way it becomes clear that Our Lord's commands can be dismissed as absurd if they are seen as calling for literal application. What however he was doing was casting a principle into an extreme picture form so as to arouse our attention. The concrete is always sharper than the abstract. The principle stands. All who profess to follow Christ are asked to give it their obedience. Seeking peace with all men, working for reconciliation, is so important in the life of a Christian, and in the life and witness of the whole Church, that should there come times when worship or reconciliation jostle for the priority, it is the worship that must give way, even though it is normally the Church's first responsibility. Jesus intended proclaiming this principle as forcibly as he could which is why he used the awkward illustration he did, 'sticking out a mile'. Reconciliation first.

Notice in the story that it is not the Churchgoer who is conscious of a grievance in his own heart. The trouble is his brother has a grievance *against him*. This is what he must put right if he can. So what we are considering here is not confession of personal sin but practical action in clearing up a complaint.

Prayer
>Lord, thou knowest how quarrels break out,
>   differences occur
>   and tempers become frayed,
>Make me, as much as lies within me,
>   a reconciling person
>   an improver of atmosphere
>   and a healer of divisions.
>So shall I be following in obedience of heart
>Thou Thyself, the eternal Prince of Peace.

THURSDAY

What love does

1 John 5.3 (NEB) For to love God is to keep his commands; and they are not burdensome,

In her autobiography *Growing Pains* (Gollancz 1977)

Daphne du Maurier records the astonishment that came over her when she found herself responding at once to an order given by a man to do something. Up to that time in her life, she confessed, she hated doing anyone's bidding, she wished above all else to be independent, to be left alone. But the man had fallen in love with her, and she was fast falling in love with him. Not long after they married. What she discovered was that she felt no resentment whatsoever in doing what he asked, she even wanted to do it, indeed more than that, she enjoyed being ordered about *by him*. It was a new experience.

The life-style which the Christian way involves can be, probably will be, resented if it is imposed. Most of us wish to shape our lives as we will, especially when we are young. When however the truth dawns on us, by whatever means, that God actually loves us, not only collectively but individually, notwithstanding our shortcomings, and wishes for nothing so much as our final happiness (for this is what the life, death and resurrection of Christ indicate) then we begin to love him in return.

And when that love is evoked what he asks of us is not resented. His commandments are not reckoned to be 'grievous' (Authorized Version) or 'burdensome' (New English Bible). We actually want to keep them. We *want* to obey.

The Christian life cannot be lived apart from this reciprocal love.

Prayer

> O Love that wilt not let me go,
> I rest my weary soul in thee:
> I give thee back the life I owe,
> That in thine ocean depths its flow
>   May richer, fuller, be.

(G. Matheson)

FRIDAY

Authority, obdience and freedom

Mark 1.22 He taught them as having authority

Jesus spoke with authority. The congregation in the Capernaum synagogue were soon aware of this when he began his preaching ministry. Authority was also evident in his dealings with individuals who sought him out with specific requests. The rich young ruler, for example, was told to sell his possessions and donate the proceeds to the poor, and the cured leper was ordered to show himself to the priest and to obtain a certificate of cleansing. Jesus did not however follow up the rich man to see if he obeyed, nor did he check on the cured leper.

There are important lessons here, not least for our day when the whole conception of authority is suspect. Authority there has to be if there is to be obedience; and obedience there has to be if there is to be allegiance. You cannot obey nothing. Jesus's disciples therefore needed Jesus's authority so that by their obedience they could show their allegiance as his disciples.

Come back now to the point that Jesus did not check on those to whom he gave instructions. There were no sanctions, no penalties for disobedience. This means that Jesus's exercise of authority did not cancel out freedom on the part of those to whom he gave orders. They could obey, they could disobey. Thus freedom coexisted with authority. So it must be if there is to be growth and development, they cannot take place in the absence of freedom.

None of this however is possible in the absence of mutual trust on the part of teacher and taught, parent and child, leader and led. The healthiest situation is when the led *wish* to obey the leader because they trust him.

To think over
> God does command 'Thou shalt', 'Thou shalt not'.
> But he also loves – sufficient to suffer for us.
> In the face of *both* command *and* love we are free to obey or to disobey,
> deciding for ourselves which is the better course to pursue.

SATURDAY

An ordinary day

Matthew 25.23 (NEB) 'You have proved trustworthy in a small way';

She had very little money. She was a student without much cash beyond her grants. Not surprisingly therefore the room where she lived was sparsely furnished; and what goods and chattels there were could only be described as cheap. The room was not however unattractive. It even possessed a certain style. There was nothing tawdry or vulgar about it. No one would label it drab. On the contrary there was colour, light and warmth. She had made the best use of the possibilities open to her.

Whether or not today turns out to be drab or enjoyable will largely depend on whether or not we make the best use of what comes our way. The day may be ordinary. Nothing exciting. Only the garden to tidy, the weekend shopping, routine household duties, an evening at home with nothing in particular 'on' (as we say). We could moan about the mediocrity. On the other hand we could build on the little we have. The ability to walk where we will, to use our hands, to see. Not everyone has these basic facilities in working order. Are we going to make the best use of today? Not tomorrow! Today. When it comes to inner satisfaction and contentment about our lot everything depends not on how much or how little we possess but on whether or not we make the best use of what we have now. We make today, it need not make us. Are we willing for obedience at this very ordinary level?

Prayer
>   Lord, I thank you for what I have
>   Help me to make the best use of it today.

SUMMARY FOR THE WEEK

Obedience

At first sight obedience seems out of place in the Christian way of life. It is all very well in the Old Testament where laws regulating the day to day life of the Hebrew people feature so prominently, but do we not read in the New Testament how 'Christ is the end of the law unto righteousness to everyone that believeth' (Romans 10.4) and that 'love is the fulfilment of the law' (Romans 13.10)? Moreover did not Jesus sum up the whole matter by answering the scribe who asked which was the first commandment of all 'Thou shalt *love* the Lord thy God . . . and Thou shalt *love* thy neighbour as thyself' (Mark 12.28–31)?

Leave the Bible on the side for a moment. Here is a thoroughly wholesome little family – father, mother, son and daughter. Not rich, not poor. Happiness reigns in that home. They have their differences. They make mistakes. But love reigns. You can tell it. No special pleading is necessary. Now where in this atmosphere does obedience fit? Its requirement is certainly not obvious because no commandments seem to be laid down at all. Yet the family has standards. But everyone seems to sense what to do. The truth must be that somehow love has transposed (not abolished) law in that place. Obedience does not have to be enforced. It is *willingly* given because the family's standards are believed in by all its members.

This is the situation the New Testament has in mind. This is how life should be in the Christian Church. This is what the Kingdom of God is like.

Two more points need to be made.

First, in the Bible obedience is almost always connected with hearing. It is the voice of the Lord that we are called to obey. But *not* first of all hearing and obeying commandments about conduct. This is not where the New Testament emphasis lies but rather on *hearing the gospel*. To obey is to listen to it. (See Romans 10.16 where the Greek word hupakouō means to answer a knock or summons and thus 'to obey'). To disobey is to shut the ears on the gospel. Thus 'to obey' almost comes to equal 'to believe'. And this brings in the element of the will. There are those who will not listen and there are those who will. Why some people will not obey, that is listen to the gospel is the 'sixty-dollar question'. Perhaps we can only look into our hearts to find an answer. The will has something to do with it, which is why we have given the title *A Willingness for Obedience* to this fourth section in our meditations.

The second point is this. In the New Testament the weight of the call to obedience is taken off us and placed instead on Christ. The commandments of God still operate in the Kingdom of God which Christ came to fulfill. His aim was not to destroy the law (see Matthew 5.17). Indeed the Sermon on the Mount appears as an even more strict application of the Old Jewish law. It is enough to make the stoutest heart quail. Who can rise to this standard? But Christ did. That is the point. He rose to it *for us*. He was obedient unto death (Philippians 2.8). 'He learned obedience by the things he suffered and so became for all those who obey him (hear him) the author (or leader) of eternal Salvation' (Hebrews 5.8–9). So through his obedience many are made righteous (that is, put in a right relation with God) See Romans 5.19. This is good news. This is the gospel of Christ. Are we willing to hear it? which being interpreted means, Are we willing for obedience?

A Christian life-style

I will go forth in the strength of the Lord God:
and will make mention of thy righteousness only.
Psalm 71.14 (BCP)

The Church's Structures

Acts 15.6 (NEB) The apostles and elders held a
meeting . . .

Today, Sunday, is the day for Christian worship.
Church buildings come into their own on the first day
of the week in a way that is not possible on
week-days. But on week-days many meetings are
arranged and much committee work embarked on in
order to make that Sunday worship in the Church
possible, and to maintain it. Not that Sunday worship
is the only service of the Church. But for this, and all
the other activity, committee work has to be. It builds
up from local parish councils to National Synods. All
of these require election to membership. There are
expense accounts, agenda papers and minutes.
Policy documents get produced. Then lobbying.
Parties are formed to sway voting. Subtle tactics are
possible, even probable. People start talking about
'nice footwork'. Of course Church committees always
begin with prayer, but this having been concluded in
a matter of minutes, the work proceeds no differently
from that in a non-Church assembly, though possibly
with a little more restraint and courtesy, though not
always. In the end decisions are made on a majority
vote, sometimes small. This is how democracy
works. Democracy is an 'in word'.

The question must be asked however, Is there a
Christian life-style for Church Committee work over

and above the restraint and the courtesy? Ought there to be? Can the Church be satisfied that having been faithful to the democratic procedure the proper course has been followed? After all the Church is not a democratic society. The apostles were not elected to their apostleships. They were called to it by Christ.

So ought there to be more 'waiting on God', more looking for the leading of the Spirit, more delay till there is something closer to a unanimity of heart and mind? The way is not easy. We are so accustomed to worldly methods. We cannot see how anything else will work. Perhaps on Sunday we ought to give more time to praying that our week-day Committee work will show a more distinctive life-style. If such were achieved it would in itself be a much needed witness to the world.

Prayer

> Lord, we pray today for our Church Councils,
>> our Deanery and Diocesan Synods
>> the National Synod
>> and other Committees of the various
>> Churches.
> Grant that not only what is decided
>> but the way it is decided
>> may be in accordance with thy Will and Spirit.
> We ask in the name of Jesus Christ our Lord.

A place for pride

Romans 12.3 (NEB) In virtue of the gift that God in his grace has given me I say to everyone among you: do not be conceited or think too highly of yourself; but think your way to a sober estimate based on the measure of faith that God has dealt to each of you.

Correggio, who was almost wholly self-taught as an artist, went one day to Rome. There he was taken to see the paintings of Raphael. For a long time he studied them, picture after picture. But he never spoke a word. After a long time when he had gone over each painting with searching eyes someone approached him with the enquiry, 'Well?' There was a long pause. Then Correggio spoke. He said, 'I too am a painter.'

There is a proper place for pride – pride in one's work. Each day's work should be done so that when the evening comes we can be proud of what we have accomplished, or at least attempted. There is something wrong with our understanding of humility if it does not leave room for *this pride*.

Pray

for those who are incapacitated for work
those who have lost the will to work,
those who through no fault of their own are out of work.

Prayer

>Lord, I thank you for my work,
>>the gifts which enable me to work,
>>the skill I have been able to bring to it
>and the rewards it has brought me.
>Give me grace never to use it for wrong ends.

TUESDAY

Courtesy and intelligence

Colossians 4.6 'Let your speech be alway with grace, seasoned with salt, that ye may know how ye ought to answer every man.'

According to St Paul there is a Christian speech-style. Certainly the Authorized Version of the Bible has accurately translated the Greek words behind this text, but they need modernizing for contemporary ears. A new Italian version has done well here. *'Parlate sempre con gentilezza e intelligenza'*. It is even slightly more arresting than the New English Bible at this point. 'Let your conversation be always gracious and never insipid'. The lesson is clear. Crude, cutting and contentious utterance is out for all who profess to follow the Christian way. Their manner of speaking should be in sharp constrast to the strident tones so common in today's protesting society. Isaiah foreshadowed as much when he told of the speech-style of God's Servant in the first of the Servant Songs (so-called) in Isaiah 42.2. Unfailing courtesy should be the hallmark of the Christian. Perhaps the television presentation of Septimus Harding (from Trollope's novel) raising his hat as he refused the offers of a prostitute on one of his unaccustomed visits to London was meant merely to raise a laugh, but there is something in it. A Christian is unfailingly courteous. It is a mark of his faith.

But there is something else. A Christian's conversation should always be intelligent. Silly, empty talking is frowned upon in the New Testament, so is gossip and mere chatter. If only the news could get around – One thing about these Christians, they do always talk sense. There is a need to train the tongue in order to acquire the Christian speech-style. None of this means that Christian conversation should be humourless for that would make it 'insipid' or 'speech without salt' the very style against which St Paul is set; but the humour must not be empty. Courtesy and intelligence then.

There is a third consideration. Study how best to talk with each person you meet. Subtle wit may be right for the scoffer's mocking question but not for the simple man or woman seeking guidance. Those who do not consider those *to whom* they are talking are inconsiderate. Such is unChristian speech however courteous, however intelligent. Talking should never take place for the talker's sake but always for the one addressed. Love would get it right.

Prayer

Set a watch, O Lord, before my lips
and guard the motives of my tongue.

Cheerfulness

Matthew 9.2 (RV) 'Son, be of good cheer'

My guess is that the man to whom Jesus addressed these words looked anything but cheerful. He was a paralytic, so stiff with paralysis he could not walk at all. He was unable even to get to Jesus for the healing it was reputed he might receive at his hands, or at his word, unless he could persuade four strong men to carry him there, or they themselves possessed sufficient pity in their hearts to volunteer for this service.

And when the task was undertaken the way into Jesus was blocked by a crowd. Not to be outdone, however, the four strong men made use of the outside stairway of the house where Jesus was, taking them up to the roof. Then, making a hole in it (it must have been sizable to take a man on a stretcher), they let down the paralytic in front of Jesus. What a way for a patient to arrive! Did Jesus laugh then? It is difficult to see how he could be human – and he was human – if he didn't laugh then. But there was no smile on the faces of the four stretcher bearers, let alone the paralytic's. Nor I guess on Peter's face because this was his house and he would have to mend the hole! But there must have been a smile on Jesus's face for his first words to the paralytic were 'Cheer up son!'. It was a favourite word of his. Jesus radiated cheerfulness. He must have done. Twelve men would not have followed him up the hill and down dale all the way from Galilee to Jerusalem had he not some tremendous buoyancy about him.

Christians ought to be characterized by cheerfulness. Not a forced back-slapping heartiness which is offensive but the innate and achieved disposition of people from whose faces in consequence a smile is never absent for long. None of us is walking in the steps of our Lord and Master if, depressed we spread gloom and despondency.

Prayer
> Lord, grant me your grace today
> to be cheerful;
> cheerful with a buoyancy
> that is deep, well-founded and infectious.

THURSDAY

Christian eyes

Philippians 4.8 (NEB) 'And now, my friends, all that is true, all that is noble, all that is just and pure, all that is lovable and gracious, whatever is excellent and admirable – fill all your thoughts with these things.'

There is much in the world that is mean and ugly, and there is much that is gracious and beautiful. There are lives that end in tragedy and there are lives that are brimful of happiness. There are people with dirty minds and there are people with noble minds. There are dunghills and there are banks of flowers, storm clouds and golden sunsets. The question is not what do we see, but on what do we *fix our eyes*. Yes, and what do we think about and talk about?

There is a Christian way of looking at the world which is neither obscurantist nor unrealistic, though these charges are made. It sees the dark, the unlovely and the tragic; and wherever people are involved, or indeed any living creature, there is sympathy (which means suffering with) and an urge to help, comfort and relieve. But because it believes in a good Creator, it has eyes cleared to see the noble, the lovable and gracious *whenever and wherever they turn up*. What people see around them is an indication of what they believe about life. Does it only exist to mock us? or is there some purpose of good in it, some divine purpose? In like manner what the Christian consistently remarks on – the ugly or the beautiful, the mean or the generous – shows up how real or unreal, how influential or uninfluential, is the faith professed.

Jesus once said, 'Take heed how you hear'. He might equally well have said 'Take heed *how you see*, and to what you draw attention.' Perhaps he did say this. Paul would not have been surprised. Hence his words to the Christians in Philippi.

Prayer

> Lord, open my eyes today
> to see the good,
>   the gracious,
>   and the admirable,
> even when others do not see;
> and to remark on it.

FRIDAY

Approachable

Philippians 2.7 Christ Jesus . . . made himself of no
reputation, and took upon him the
form of a servant, and was made in
the likeness of men.

A young pastor in Germany, having completed his
training was anxious to work in a city parish.
Unfortunately no city parish was vacant at the time,
only a rural one; so he, wife and child, set off for the
country. Not surprisingly perhaps, he made little
headway as a village pastor. 'He doesn't fit in here'
said the parishioners. 'I don't belong here' said the
pastor. And so there built up a great wall between
pastor and people. Then the pastor's child fell
seriously ill, and after a time, died, making the whole
situation more difficult to bear. To the pastor's
astonishment however, he found he had come much
closer to the people and they to him. It was as if the
invisible wall had been dismantled. The people said

'He too, is a man like us'. No longer did they see him as 'the man up there in the pulpit', nor write him off as a 'city type'. They discovered that they had as their pastor a wounded man. And now that he too was dependent on the mercy of God they felt that he was a human shepherd of their souls who could be trusted.

Christ Jesus took the form of a servant 'being born in the likeness of man'. No longer was God 'up there' or 'out there'. He never had been but when people saw Jesus in the rough and tumble of this world, and came to understand who he was, they knew for certain. So he is qualified to be our shepherd.

St Paul however, when he incorporated these words in Philippians 2.7ff from an old Christian hymn, did not stop there. He said the same mind should be in all Christian people as was in Christ Jesus. We should not stand on our dignity. We should not be aloof. Christians must always be approachable people. The lesson applies in the office and workshop as well as in the home.

Prayer

    Thou didst leave thy throne and thy kingly crown
    When thou camest to earth for me; . .
    O come to my heart, Lord Jesus;
    There is room in my heart for Thee.

                (Emily E S Elliot)
                (Hymn A & M (R) 363)

Charitable

Mark 9.40 (NEB) For he who is not against us is on our side.

Some of us find it easier to be charitable about people's wrong action than about their wrong thinking, wrong that is from our point of view. We look for excuses for the former in their harsh unbringing or frustrating circumstances. But what about those who profess to be Christians and yet deviate from the traditional and orthodox interpretation of faith? Will our charity extend to them?

There took place an incident in the life of Jesus which has something to say on this. The disciples saw a man carrying out works of healing in Christ's name but he did not belong to their group. So they felt sure he must be wrong, so sure they asked leave of Christ to stop him forthwith.

But the man was working *in Christ's name*. This is what the disciples failed to grasp. Instead they concentrated on the fact that he was not working in the way they worked, he was not a member of their company. Jesus however regarded him with charity. 'Do not stop him' he said 'no one who does a work of divine power *in my name* will in the same breath be able to speak evil of me. For he who is not against us is on our side'. His charity indeed extended to an almost unbelievable limit. 'I tell you this; if anyone gives you a cup of water to drink because you are followers of the Messiah, that man assuredly will not go unrewarded'.

Prayer

> Lord, give me grace to hold fast to my faith, but grace also to be charitable to those who express it differently.

SUMMARY FOR THE WEEK

The Christian life-style

In 1976 the then Archbishop of Canterbury, at a time of considerable national unease and dissatisfaction, launched what came to be called his 'Call to the Nation'. He asked two leading questions. 'What kind of society do we want?' and 'What sort of persons ought we to be?'. As a suggestion for answering the second question, he advocated three characteristics. We should put God first, our neighbour second, and self last. In simple terms, perhaps too simple, it nevertheless fairly delineated the Christian life-style.

First, putting God first. The Christian does this visibly when he is seen making his way to Church to worship on the first day of the week. To be known as a Churchgoer is the most obvious indication of a distinctive life-style whenever, wherever, Church-going is out of fashion. God is also put first where a place is allotted to private prayer. It is acknowledging that the control of our fortunes and our destinies is not entirely in our hands. Therefore we commit

75

ourselves, our joys, our sorrows and our concerns, as well for others as for ourselves, into the care and keeping of a divine Sovereign Lord whose we are and whom we serve. And when it comes to conduct the decisive question is not, 'What can I get out of this?'; or, 'Is this what everyone expects of me?', but, 'Is what I propose doing right or wrong in God's sight?'. This is putting God first. It is irrefutable evidence of the Christian life-style.

Secondly, putting our neighbour second, we ought to begin with those closest to us, that is to say, not merely next door, but in our own home. There is not much to be said for giving handsome donations to relieve poverty on the other side of the world and at the same time being a 'pain in the neck' to live with at home. Consideration for the feelings, fears and inner hopes of those with whom we 'rub shoulders' every day is the place for good neighbourliness to begin. There is, in fact, a Christian life-style for the home, and one of the marks is appreciation, the very antithesis of taking everything for granted. But the members of our families, and the people in the flat upstairs are not our sole neighbours. Anyone of any class, colour or creed who is in need is our neighbour. The Christian life-style includes at least a sensitive awareness of all such, but where the opportunity arises, or can be made, it stretches forth a helping hand. It does not 'pass by on the other side.'

Thirdly, self is put last. This is such a reversal of the common practice that it is striking, and a man and woman who habitually acts in this fashion is likely to be dubbed 'something of a saint'. Circumstances, favourable or unfavourable, have nothing to do with it. There are moving stories of prisoners-of-war in pitiful poverty and pain giving their little to others in worse plight than themselves. There are people in what is called 'high society' who are 'thoughtful' for those whose duty it is to serve them. The Christian life-style is kind, considerate and humble. It is never arrogant, hurtful or boasting. Intellectual eminence is not necessary to produce it, nor is it the natural outcome of a limited education. Putting self last derives from the following of Christ who, though first in personal excellence, was willing to be last in precedence, taking the place of a servant.

There is nothing like the Christian life-style in all the world. It is likely to be trampled on but nothing will receive a greater reward in the eternal reckoning, though that is the last thing it seeks.

Trials and tribulations

God is our hope and strength:
a very present help in trouble
Psalm 46.1 (BCP)

THE FIFTH SUNDAY IN LENT

Safe self-denial

Mark 8.34,35 If any man would come after me, let him deny himself, and take up his cross, and follow me. For whosoever would save his life shall lose it.

The passion of Christ is the traditional theme for this Sunday's worship. We are to follow Christ *in his passion*. We are to take up our cross. We are to deny ourselves. This is a proper Lenten summons.

Self-denial however, like many religious exercises can become self-centred. Then it is virtually worthless. Tolstoy has a striking illustration of this in his novel *Resurrection*. Nekhlyudov, finding a servant girl called Maslova attractive, got her with child. Turned out of her employers' house in consequence, she drifted into brazen-fraced prostitution. Discovering this, Nekhlyudov was tormented by his guilt and went to enormous pains to make amends. He tracked her down to filthy prisons, and even followed her into exile, offering marriage 'to make her respectable'. But she refused. She saw through his eagerness to atone. He wanted to feel comfortable again. He was concerned for the salvation of his own soul. In truth, it was not for Maslova that he cared, only for himself.

Self-denial can place self in the centre of our own picture. We can pride ourselves on what we are giving up. We can imagine that we are making great strides in the Christian life, even saving our own souls. We like this. It gives us inner satisfaction. We enjoy the spiritual comfort our mortification provides.

The truth is self-denial is not safe unless it is self-giving (Read Mark 8.34,35 again noting the striking juxtaposition of the two verses). Self-giving is costly, more costly than giving either time or money.

Prayer
>Lord, you gave yourself for us.
>Help us who follow you
>to give ourselves to other people.
>Let this be our self-denial.

MONDAY

Medicine for sores

Luke 16.20 'full of sores'

We don't like this picture of the man in the parable which Jesus told, but some of us are full of sores, and there must be few who know nothing of sores. There is the sore which still hurts, come about by a cared-for friend who died prematurely. There is the sore resulting from some let-down by a work mate whom we thought we could trust. There is that sore every time we recall what a fool we made of ourselves by what we unthinkingly did last month – or was it really unthinkingly – but it seems like last week, it rankles so. And for some the terrible, terrible sore which takes so long to heal, if ever it does – a marriage break.

Is there any ointment for these sores? any medicine to heal them? Let us be frank. No, not easily. But there is love. It is the only effective remedy. We have to lay hold of the eternal reality that God loves us, sores and all, even loves us *because* of our sores. Then they do not fester; and this is always the trouble with sores, they tend to fester. With this ointment however, in time they heal, with only the marks left, if that. Admittedly an effort is required to grasp the love of God for insignificant mortals like us, and consistent effort, but it was there in the ministry of Jesus as a pointer. And sometimes we come to it through the love of other people who surprisingly enough love us, warts and all. This is the medicine. It really is.

'He healeth those that are broken in heart:
and giveth medicine to heal their sickness'.

(Ps 147.3 BCP)

Prayer
> Lord, help me to accept your love of me, even of me.

The experience of failure

1 Kings 19.4 (NEB) 'Lord, take my life, for I am no better than my fathers before me.'

People do exist whose lives appear, even on close examination, to be a series of successes. Good home. Examination firsts. A chosen career. Steady promotion. A happy marriage. Good health. More than adequate income. Honours. Names could be supplied. For most of us however life is not like that. We know the taste of failure.

There is failure in school examinations. Failure to find a job. Marriage failure. A girl may feel herself a failure because she is single, made more hurtful by insensitive remarks of people who ought to know better, alas, some of them parents. There is failure to 'get along' with someone at work in spite of trying. And failure in business. And the failure of health and strength in old age.

Before we write ourselves off as 'no good' because of our failures let us remember that in the Bible he who stands (in a way) for all the prophets – Elijah – once prayed to God to take away his life, he felt such a failure. And the career of one of the greatest of the prophets if not *the* greatest – Jeremiah – was a failure from start to finish. And when Jesus asked his disciples whom people thought he was, they replied, some say Jeremiah.

So God doesn't write off the people who know the bitter taste of failure. He actually loves them and uses them. He can do this because they are not insulated from him by reason of their successful self-sufficiency. No one enjoys failure, but the loss is never total if we can grasp *how God sees the failures*, and begin again from there.

Prayer
> Lord, when I fail to believe in myself
> and am down;
> that you still believe in me
> lifts me up
> so that I can make my way.
> Help me, Lord.

WEDNESDAY

Tight corners

Acts 26.22 (NEB) But I had God's help, and so to this very day I stand

St Paul was in a tight corner when he gave this testimony to God's sustaining power. Standing there in the dock, no doubt with a clanking chain on his wrist, flanked by prison warders, and all under the eyes of a royal couple, flaunting their pomp and fickleness, he dared to divulge his faith, risking their ridicule.

Some of us have been in tight corners. Who has *not* at some time been in a tight corner? Not maybe like St

Paul before judges bent on obtaining a conviction –
though prisoners of conscience in modern oppressive
regimes must not be forgotten – but there was that
sick bed from which we reckoned we never would
rise. We had God's help then and so to this very day
we stand. There were those months agonizing how to
raise that mortgage; would we ever emerge from the
depressing restriction of that tight corner? – but we
did. There was that time when every finger of
condemnation would seem legitimately to point in
our direction as the cause of breakdown in those
business negotiations, though we were innocent
enough. And which of us who has lived sufficiently
long to know what the heartbreak of bereavement is
like can forget how we doubted if ever we would
laugh again – but we have. We had God's help and to
this very day we stand.

Life is not a smooth affair, not even a man or woman
as dedicated in God's service as was St Paul. God
does not guide his servants past all the bunkers, all
the scrapes, all the frightening set-backs. If we do not
know this already from experience we may learn it in
the next twenty-four hours. But we need not panic.
At the end of the day we shall be able to say with St
Paul 'But I had God's help, and so to this day I stand.'

Thought of the day

    O God, our help in ages past,
    Our hope for years to come,
    Our shelter from the stormy blast,
    And our eternal home:
                 (Hymns A & M (R) 165) (I Watts)

Tunnels

Acts 27.20 (NEB) For days on end there was no sign of
either sun or stars,

The longest tunnel in the world, the Seikan, linking
two Japanese islands of Honshu and Hokkaido, a
distance of twenty-two miles, was begun in 1975.
Perhaps one day England and France will be connected by a tunnel.

Sometimes our lives run into a sort of tunnel. We find
ourselves in the dark, closed in with nothing to see
except the tunnel walls. This may happen in bereavement when we lose someone very close and dear to
us. Another kind of tunnel may be a mountain of
work to be 'got through' (as we say). Losing hold of
the certainties of our faith, or what we thought were
our certainties (and this can happen to the most
saintly people) really is like entering a black tunnel.
Then there is illness, a severe illness, perhaps
terminal; the sick-room, the nursing, the pills and the
drip-feed constitute all there is of life. Compared with
the normal freedom of living, this is a grim tunnel.
And there are threatening circumstances, such as a
storm at sea, the sort of situation described in Acts
Chapter 27, the account of St Paul's voyage to Rome.

Tunnels are never entered for the mere sake of
entering them; nor are they constructed for fun.
Tunnels are bored – and the art of constructing them
has advanced considerably in the twentieth century –

in order to enable progress to be made to a desired destination otherwise blocked off, probably by mountains or by sea. To reach the destination however it is essential *to keep going* in the tunnel, to stop half way is fatal.

So with tunnels of life. If we persevere through them in the faith that they lead somewhere, that is have a purpose, we shall discover sooner or later that they have brought us to an inner strength of character not otherwise to be attained. And if the analogy of the tunnel does not appear to square with a *terminal* illness, we need to remember that in our faith we hold to the belief that at the end of *this* tunnel is the glorious light of the resurrection life.

Prayer
> When the way is dark
> and the dreary days loom like a tunnel,
> Lord, help me to persevere with the journey,
> confident that light will shine at the end.

FRIDAY

Secrets

Psalm 44.21 (BCP) He (God) knoweth the very secrets of the heart.

There can't be many people, if any at all, who have no secrets of the heart; longings, hopes, fears, loves, hates, things done of which we are ashamed. They stretch right across the board of life's span. Youth has secret ambitions, private temptations. And young men and women and some not so young, have secret loves, sometimes a passion which burns inside, both attractive and repelling, liberating and restricting. Then there are antipathies, bottled up jealousies and crude hidden resentments. Older people have secret fears of illness, of cancer, heart attacks, bereavements and a lonely old age. No one knows. We don't talk about these things. We can't. But they make their mark all the time on the course our lives take. There is a strain, loss of freedom, and no real peace.

What can be done? We can lay hold of this – that God knows the secrets of our hearts. He knows them better than we know them. He knows what our nearest and dearest do not know. And we can ask for cleansing of those secrets. No, not the publishing of them all, that might be most unwise, but the cleansing. Then the weight is lifted. And without the weight of the secrets of the heart life runs more easily, it really does.

Prayer

> Almighty God, unto whom all hearts are open,
> all desires known, and from whom no secrets
> are hid: Cleanse the thoughts of our hearts
> by the inspiration of thy Holy Spirit, that
> we may perfectly love thee, and worthily
> magnify thy holy Name; through Christ our
> Lord, Amen.

(BCP)

SATURDAY

Driven off course

Psalm 66.11 (BCP) We went through fire and water, and thou broughtest us out into a wealthy place.

In the violence of a storm at sea a ship may be driven off course. The construction of the ship is not to be blamed, the winds and the waves were too much for it. Nor is the captain necessarily at fault, he did all within his capacity to keep his vessel on the shipping lane where his compass told him he should be. Not until the storm abated, hopefully with no irreparable damage done, could the ship get back on course and continue its voyage.

Sometimes sincere and dedicated Christian people get blown off course. No wise onlooker will rush in to apportion blame. Perhaps the odds against their faith were too great. Rationalism can be very compelling. Perhaps gusty winds of sexual temptation suddenly caught him/her off balance lifting the normally controlled person off their feet. Perhaps the dull round of disappointment lasted too long, or health failing too drastically, drove the heart close to the rocks of shattering depression.

Who is there who hasn't at some time or other been driven off course in the day to day journey through life? We have not been what we know we ought to be. Do not react too harshly. Do not be too ready to blame. The one thing needful is to get back on course again. Be sure of this. It is the nature of storms to blow themselves out. The sun will shine again.

Prayer
> When I am driven by the fierceness of the winds, and the lights in my ship have gone out; Lord, guide me through the darkness and bring me back on course.

SUMMARY FOR THE WEEK

Suffering

Christians have to face the awkward fact that suffering, indeed the sheer weight of the vast volume of suffering since the world began, is an embarrassment to faith in God, especially a God of love. Christian faith does not initially ease the problem of suffering, it makes it worse. The complaint which runs as follows has not lost its force. Either God is unable to elimate the suffering of mankind – in which case he cannot be God; or he will not – in which case he cannot be a God of love. It is no wonder some people seek a refuge from the problem in agnosticism or atheism. The admission has to be made that we have no final solution.

This does not imply however that there is no more to be said. We cannot wrap the subject up and stow it away in the cupboard to become a kind of skeleton. We cannot even lodge it in the pending file, perhaps at the bottom. Suffering is a fact of life. We cannot dodge it. And in the midst of history stands the cross of Christ which surely must be saying something if the suffering man there was really the word of God made flesh.

What does it say? For one thing that God does not will suffering, he does not inflict it. In Isaiah 63.9 is an arresting statement about God and his relation to the suffering of people. 'In all their affliction he was afflicted.' This involvement of God in human pain actually became visible that first Good Friday to all who were willing to believe that God was in Christ on the cross of Calvary. And the cross still stands conveying the same message. God shares in the sufferings of this world. This is the kind of God he is.

What else does the cross of Christ say about suffering? A hard lesson, perhaps, and easily misunderstood; – suffering arises from rebellion *against* God. In AD 29, or whatever is the date of the crucifixion, the decision was publicly made and popularly supported that this Jesus of Nazareth must be liquidated (to use a modern phrase), and that in the most summary and repulsive fashion. This is a historical fact, but it is more; the rejection of Christ is a mirror in which is reflected the age-long rebellion of mankind as a whole against the idea of God as the Creator and Lord of the Universe. It has no creator, it has no lord, no lord, that is, except man who can do with it as he wills. This rebellion, says the cross of Christ, must result in suffering. Not (let the point be made plainly) that all individual suffering is the direct outcome of individual rebellion. There are innocent sufferers by the thousands. The lesson to be learned from the cross of Christ is that we are all, everyone of us, in the boat of the rebellious human race, whether relatively innocent or not, and that means suffering as a fact of human life. We may have to encounter suffering ourselves because we belong, just as a whole family suffers if one member 'goes off the rails'.

If this is true, and it looks uncommonly like it, yet the whole explanation of suffering does not lie here. How could it? How could rebellion against God be made in any way responsible for the pain caused, for instance, by an earthquake in Southern Italy? or a lifeboat capsizing off the Devon coast in a freak storm? Surely these calamities show *nature* inflicting suffering. And we have all heard of nature 'red in tooth and claw'. Is pain and suffering then a constituent part of the evolutionary process of nature? Life does not even begin without pain. Every mother knows it. Does every upward thrust then into new life, does every development of life, does every continuance of life involve struggle? and struggle means suffering. Is this why suffering is *a fact of life*. If so, be it noted Christ entered that struggle.

In so far then as we have sought for the cause of suffering we have considered the rebelliousness of man against God and the evolutionary process of nature. A third ground has been sought in the existence of an evil force personalized under the name of the Devil or Satan. If this requires belief in a kind of Dualism so that God is not the sole Creator and sustainer of the Universe, it must be rejected as an explanation. On the other hand it has to be admitted that evil has from time to time, not least in the twentieth century, taken on such ghastly forms, that the existence of some spiritual evil force at work in the world does not seem improbable, indeed it might seem to be sufficient explanation. We find we cannot do without words like satanic, diabolical and devilish to express the enormity of some of the wickedness perpetrated. From the gospel accounts it appears that Jesus had to struggle against such a spiritual enemy.

Must our speculations end here? Is there nothing positive to say? Yes, there is. The cross of Christ declares that suffering need not be waste material. Indeed in the hands of God it is not waste material. Rather it is the means by which rebellious mankind is brought into peace and harmony with the Creator. There never has been any more powerful instrument for changing people's attitudes than the suffering Christ on the cross of Calvary. This does not make suffering anything but bad in itself, and no stone must be left unturned to try and alleviate it, nor must cooperation be shunned with everyone whoever he may be, and whatever his motives, who engages in this ministry of compassion. Nevertheless God is able to bring good out of this bad thing. It is here, supremely here, that the power of God is manifested. God is able to make all things serve his purposes, even pain. This is something his omnipotence certainly means.

What then must be the distinctive practical Christian

contribution to the fact of suffering? *First* and foremost to withhold no effort to relieve it wherever possible. *Secondly* to avoid the pessimistic conclusion that the whole of life has been ruined by suffering. This is not true. Beauty and pleasure abound in this world appreciated by far more than the inhabitants of sophisticated societies. God's is a splendid creation. *Thirdly* to have nothing to do with ideas of an impersonal Fate capriciously moving us about as playthings for its own grim pleasure. *Fourthly* not to glamorize suffering on the false understanding that it always ennobles. It does not. Sometimes it dehumanizes. *Fifthly* not to impose suffering on ourselves supposing that thereby we shall become heroic martyrs. We may not. We may become instead a liability to all we meet. *Sixthly* to avoid joining the all-too-popular demand to ferret out those responsible for some particular calamity and to bring them to justice, supposing that when this has been done, and may be rightly done, the requirements of the situation have been met. They have not. *Seventhly* there is the need to bring us all into a state of peace and harmony with God whether through pain or otherwise. When this is experienced we shall be more ready to seek peace and reconciliation in a warring world, and this is one of the major ministries of all Christians at all times.

It has to be admitted that we have no final solution to the problem of suffering. Nevertheless we follow in the steps of Jesus who did not explain why a man was born blind when the disciples asked him (see John 9.2), but who did at once proceed to heal him.

Holy Week
The Saviour

My strength is dried up like a potsherd,
and my tongue cleaveth to my gums:
and thou shalt bring me into the dust of death.

Psalm 22.15 (BCP)

King of peace

Ephesians 2.13,14,16,17 (NEB)

> But now in union with Christ Jesus you who were once far off have been brought near through the shedding of Christ's blood. For he is himself our peace. Gentiles and Jews, he has made the two one . . . This was his purpose, to reconcile the two in a single body to God through the cross, on which he killed the enmity. . . . peace to you who were far off, and peace to those who were near by;

During the Second World War a German lance-corporal on the Russian front crept forward on patrol during a pause in the gunfire. He could barely see in the grey light of early morning. Warily he kept his finger on the trigger of his weapon. At the very same moment a Russian soldier lying opposite him released the safety catch on his machine gun as he too pushed aside the undergrowth. Both German and Russian raised their heads together. Both presented each other with precisely the same sight – the face of the enemy. The lance-corporal (and it is from him that the story comes) knew that he must shoot at once. But he hesitated. He had fired his gun countless times, but always at a great mass of nameless men, the anonymous enemy: never, since the beginning of the war, at a man who lay only a pace away from him, a man full of life and strength like himself, a man who was the creation of God. He bent his finger over the trigger. But the Russian held up his hand. With a quick movement he made the sign of the cross. And the lance-corporal likewise with a quick movement raised his hand and made the sign of the cross. In the thick of that terrible conflict, which continued, somehow the cross of Christ killed the enmity between these two men separated by an enormous gulf. For a moment in the war there was peace.

It is easy to talk glibly about peace as if the achievement of it were easy. This won't do. Peace is a costly business involving sacrifice; the Cross of Christ is the evidence. So Christ is the king of peace as is no other. He began to demonstrate what he stood for on that triumphal ride (as we call it) into Jerusalem on Palm Sunday mounted on a humble donkey and not a war horse. And St Luke tells us (Luke 19.41,42) that 'when he came in sight of the city, he wept over it and said' "If only you had known, on this great day, the way that leads to peace!"'.

A thought for today

Peace perfect peace in this dark world of sin?
the blood of Jesus whispers peace within.
(*Bishop E H Bickersteth*)

Our qualified leader

Hebrews 2.10 (NEB)

> It was clearly fitting that God for whom and through whom all things exist should, in bringing many sons to glory, make the leader who delivers them perfect through sufferings.

In her novel *Voices on the Wind* (1985) Evelyn Anthony draws a vivid picture of nineteen-year-old Kate standing up to the almost brutal training in Scotland for work with the French Resistance during World War II. Her stomach turned over as the day when she would be landed in Nazi occupied France drew near. There was one comfort. Her leader would be the famous Dulac renowned for having survived untold hardships and risks in accomplishing his dangerous mission. Kate felt safe with such a leader.

This is the kind of leader we have in Jesus, a man *qualified* (it is what the word 'perfect' means in the text above) to lead because of what he went through; and the reference is not only to his Crucifixion but to much else besides. God purposed to bring his 'many sons to glory' not by some fiat of his from heaven, but by means of a representative, and that representative a leader. He would have to be visible, he would have to be attractive, and he would have to know what it is to be 'up against it' in life, and yet not give way. Moses was that kind of leader. So was Jesus.

What this implies is salvation by inspiration, even admiration. Let the theologians complain that it represents a thin doctrine of salvation. Maybe, but it is not to be despised. Admiration of Jesus as a leader qualified because he faced life the hard way, and did not weaken, is no bad place to begin Holy Week, or for that matter our discipleship altogether. Did not his Twelve disciples start just here?

Prayer

> Lord Jesus Christ,
> I see you as the strong man
>   the unflinching man
>   but also the caring man
>   the understanding man.
> Give me of your strength
>   to follow you to your Cross
>   to bear my own cross
>   and not to give way.
> So you will be my salvation.

TUESDAY IN HOLY WEEK

Our great high priest

Hebrews 7.26–8.1 (RSV)

> For it was fitting that we should have
> such a high priest, holy, blameless,
> unstained, separated from sinners,
> exalted above the heavens. He has no
> need, like those high priests, to offer

sacrifices daily, first for his own sins and then for those of the people; he did this once for all when he offered up himself. Indeed, the law appoints men in their weakness as high priests, but the word of the oath, which came later than the law, appoints a Son who has been made perfect for ever. Now the point in what we are saying is this: we have such a high priest . . . .

Yesterday we thought of Jesus as a kind of super-Moses (if the roughness of the expression will be pardoned), a super-leader. Today we think of him as a super-Aaron, he is the great high priest. This is striking. Jesus was brought before Caiaphas, the high priest, and condemned to death for blasphemy. But who was the real high priest? Who was the one who provided access for all men to God? – because that is what a priest is for. Not Caiaphas! But Christ did. Christ does. Starting from where we are 'he opened the kingdom of heaven to all believers', as the Te Deum puts it. He represents us to God.

A priest offers sacrifice in order to gain access to God. This is taken for granted the world over, but especially in Hebrew thought. So what did Jesus offer? It is a proper question if he is to be looked on as the great high priest. He offered himself. His life was poured out on the Cross. It was no blemished offering. He had consistently lived out God's will.

It is possible that these sacrificial categories of thought will make little appeal to modern half-secularized man. But the value of seeing Jesus as the great high priest in Holy Week is that all too easily we seem him *only as the victim*; the victim maybe of social injustice, religious bigotry, professional jealousy, racial hatred and downright treachery. There is truth in this. Jesus was indeed a victim. But this is less than half the truth. He was also the operator. He was opening up the way of access to God for all of us. He was, he is in fact, our *great high priest*.

> Salvation's giver, Christ the only Son,
> By that his cross and blood the victory won,
> Offered was he for greatest and for least:
> Himself the victim and himself the priest.
>
> *(7th century Trans. J M Neale)*

Prayer

> Praise be to thee O Christ
> for this unspeakable gift.

WEDNESDAY IN HOLY WEEK

Our sinbearer

1 Peter 2.22–24 (NEB)

> He committed no sin, he was convicted of no falsehood; when he was abused he did not retort with abuse, when he suffered he uttered no threats, but committed his cause to the One who judges justly. In his own person he carried our sins to the gallows, so that we might cease to live for sin and begin

101

to live for righteousness. By his wounds
you have been healed.

This description will not allow us to be satisfied with
a description of Jesus as a social, much less a political
reformer. There have been, there are still, honourable
men and women in these callings, but could the claim
possibly be made that their hands are wholly clean?
that they have never lied (always with the highest
motives of course!)? that abusive language and
threats have never passed their lips? Are not protest
and confrontation the order of the day?

No, it is not possible to categorize Jesus as a social or
political reformer though reforms in plenty, both
social and political, have stemmed from his life and
work. Jesus operated at a deeper level. He was
concerned with sin, that is original sin; (so-called),
the strange quirk in human nature that makes it tend
to take the lower moral path when it knows quite well
what is the higher, the drag in every human spirit
that makes going down hill morally far easier than
going uphill. There can be little hope of lasting reform
in any sphere of life unless the human problem is
tackled *at this level*. And not only is there original sin,
but individual sins, be they transgression of the
moral law or failures to live up to our own best
standards. Time and time again we 'miss the mark'.
The truth is we are sinners, but Christ came to our aid
as such, and went to his Cross to complete his healing
mission.

'By his wounds you have been healed' wrote the
author of the above text. But we are not made

righteous overnight. This is a false view of our salvation. Rather 'in his own person he carried our sins to the gallows, so that we might cease to live for sin and *begin to live for righteousness*'.

Prayer
> Jesus, that pardoning grace to find,
> I too would come to thee;
> O merciful to all mankind,
> be merciful to me.

(G W Briggs, 1875–1959)

MAUNDY THURSDAY

Effective remembrance

Luke 22.19 This do in remembrance of me.

This is the day when Christ sat down for his last supper with his twelve disciples. In a matter of hours he was suffering that horrible, yet wonderful death by crucifixion outside Jerusalem's walls. Horrible because no more cruel device for killing has been devised by man than the cross, wonderful because he chose not to escape it (which was possible), but to suffer it in obedience to the will of God for our salvation.

As close to that killing as time and place would allow Jesus at that last supper took bread and broke it saying 'This do in remembrance of me'. Likewise with a cup of wine poured out. Clearly he was providing for a re-enactment in ritual form of the crucifixion soon to take place. The identification could scarcely be closer when he broke the bread and said 'This is my body', and when he poured out the wine and said 'This is my blood'. As then the sacrificial death on the cross was for our redemption so must this remembrance be. The supper and the crucifixion are linked as one comprehensive event.

The word 'remembrance' is significant. To remember someone is not a mere psychological act as in our modern Western way of thinking. In the Bible it is usually connected with someone's name, and means keeping that person's life and work alive so that it is still effective. Correspondingly forgetting or rubbing someone's name out means destroying their life and work. Remembering therefore *does* something. It achieves something. There are results from remembering.

When therefore Jesus said 'Do this in remembrance of me' he was not instituting the Holy Communion as a mere reminder of what took place in the Upper Room lest the historical event be lost with the passing of time. He was giving us a ritual act which *does* something, it makes the Cross and Passion redemptive for us. No wonder the Holy Communion is the Church's central act of worship.

Prayer

> Jesus, we thus obey
> thy last and kindest word;
> here in thine own appointed way
> we come to meet the Lord.

Our hearts are open wide
to make the Saviour room;
and lo, the Lamb and crucified,
the sinners' friend is come.

(Charles Wesley)

GOOD FRIDAY

The new road

Hebrews 10.19,20 (NEB)

> So now, my friends, the blood of Jesus
> makes us free to enter boldly into the
> sanctuary by the new, living way which
> he has opened for us through the
> curtain, the way of his flesh.

The writer of these two verses wants us to think of
what Jesus did on Good Friday under the figure of a
new road being opened up. This is not difficult for us.
A number of new roads, motor ways, have been laid
down during the last ten years reducing journeying
times enormously and providing more ready access
to more places.

Jesus by living the kind of life we have to live in a
mortal body, what the text calls 'his flesh', opened up
a new road to God. He opened it for us. Roads are not
easily constructed. Nor are they cheap. Every new
road entails an enormous amount of labour. There is
in fact a vast disparity between the task of making the
road and the smooth, almost effortless drive in a car

along it afterwards. Jesus laboured hard to contruct the new road to God. It cost him his life, his life's blood. His very flesh was torn apart in the doing of it. But he achieved it. By comparison our use of that road is simple.

And now we are invited to use it. How? By looking to Christ with sympathy, admiration and trust. As simple as that. It is this attitude of heart, mind and will which gets us up on to the new road. And where does it lead? To God certainly, but not merely to the entry point into the divine presence, where we hesitate with fear and trembling, but into the divine presence itself where we encounter receptiveness, forgiveness and love.

It is not for nothing that down through the centuries men and women have knelt before a cross or crucifix as they have sought to meet with God in prayer. These symbols are reminders of the new and living way which is now open. There is nothing to stop us from drawing near. Indeed there is everything to encourage us. We are all welcome.

Prayer

Thou art the Way, the Truth, the Life;
Grant us that way to know,
That truth to keep, that life to win,
Whose joys eternal flow.

(*Bishop G W Doane*)

Tasting death for everyone

Hebrews 2.9 (RSV)

> But we see Jesus, who for a little while was made lower than the angels, crowned with glory and honour, because of the suffering of death, so that by the grace of God he might taste death for everyone.

The graveyard and the crematorium are so final. That is their terror. We shall not return from our journey thither. And what is as poignant is the fact that neither will those loved ones whom we accompanied in the funeral procession. They are dead. We cringe before the word. Dead. We try to soften it with substitutes. Our effort is the measure of our fear. Let us be honest. We are afraid.

Jesus did not skirt around this hurting part of our human experience. He wept at a graveside, and he was put in a grave himself. It is difficult to see how God in Christ can be said to go all the way with us in our lives if these two events did not take place. But they are provocative. How could death make any impact on Jesus if the life that was in him was the life of God? God cannot die. Yet the four gospels are at pains to tell us that he *was put in a grave*. He was dead on the Saturday following Good Friday. So in Christ the divine really did taste death. The statement sounds fantastic. But what can we do? Jesus was buried and we believe him to be divine.

All that we can say is that the death and burial of Jesus must have taken place *for our sakes*. They are two of the great evidences of God's grace. In Christ God did the unthinkable *for us*. So there is a gospel, a proclamation of good news, in this Holy Saturday. Of course it will be crowned with Easter, crowned by the Resurrection. Then we shall see what 'tasting death for every man' really means. But the tears associated with death cannot be wholly wiped away in this life. Christian faith does not erase bereavement. So let us keep Holy Saturday when Jesus lay in the grave, and the women who loved were weeping, and the disciples cowering away in bewiderment. It says God knows, God understands and – dare we say it? – God feels.

Prayer

> Lord, I believe
> > I believe in the resurrection of the dead
> > I believe in the life eternal
> I make these confessions in the Creed on Sundays.
> But I am afraid of dying
> > afraid of bereavement
> > afraid of loneliness.
> Give me the strength of your presence
> when I feel these experiences.
> I dare to believe you will.

The Saviour

The fundamental spiritual question for everyone of us is – how can we make ourselves acceptable to God? How can we come into his holy presence? We are sinners. We know we are. We may excuse ourselves. We may argue that our sinfulness is only relative in comparison with some of the world's notorious tyrants, tycoons and terrorists (and with justification), or even in comparison with that mediocre man next door. But the uncertainty will not go away. We are not fit to enter the divine presence. So what is to be done about it?

Perhaps we can't do anything about it. Perhaps we are unable to make ourselves acceptable to God. This sounds an appalling conclusion, but it happens to be the verdict of the Bible on our human condition. Of course there are people who disbelieve it. They reckon they are perfectly capable of running up a moral credit balance with God. What is more aren't there some people who are so good that a proportion of their moral credit can be made available for our benefit? Isn't that what the saints are for? But there is no warrant for this in scripture.

Our situation however is not hopeless. Quite the reverse. There is the Saviour Jesus Christ the Lord. Herein lies the good news. Herein is the gospel. The Saviour however is surprising. There is in fact no Saviour like him because he appears as if he himself is lost. We see him hanging limp upon a cross the victim of man's evil machinations. Why does Christ save us like this? Why does goodness have to be trampled on to bring us home to God? Why couldn't we be presented instead with a noble life ending in the tranquility of old age to inspire us all to strive harder in imitation of this wonderful example? Why this awful crucifixion? We can only suppose it was because nothing less could begin the deal with the enormity of the human problem, the appalling weight of the world's sin of which cruelty is only one frightening aspect.

But how does the death of Christ deal with human sin? Are we to see here some kind of transaction? A number of theories of the atonement (so-called) have been propounded down through the Christian centuries. Perhaps none of them explain the mystery satisfactorily, and we must always remember that men and women are saved by the Atonement not by any specific theory about it. Nevertheless we cannot adopt too superior an attitude. People have been helped to trust the Saviour sometimes by most unsatisfactory theories. There was an idea that God wanted to forgive our sins but he could only do so if satisfaction were paid to the authority of the moral law. The situation was met therefore by letting the penalty of sin fall on the innocent Jesus. So he suffered in our place, as our substitute. But this makes God a kind of tyrant, as if he must have his pound of flesh. As a theory it will not do. There was another idea that the merits of Christ's holy life, culminating in this sacrificial death, get transferred to us sinners by means of the exercise of our faith. But this is a moral figment. It implies that we are made to appear righteous when in fact we are not.

A better way is to see Christ as our representative. He is the real man. He is man as man should be, faithful, obedient and loyal to God, doing his will at all times at great cost throughout all his days; not swerving, not faltering even though it cost him his life. Christ is God's faithful servant achieving what we do not achieve, and he stands *for us*, he is our representative *before God*. We hide in him and God sees us through him. So the hymn

> Look Father, look on his anointed face,
> And only look on us as found in him:
>
> *(W Bright)*

How do we 'hide in him'? By trusting him. By exercising our faith in him. By deciding for him. What this means is that we are accepted, sinful though we are, because we die *in Christ*. We stand in a new relationship to God because of what God in Christ has done. Our situation is different from what it would have been without the life and work of Christ. He is our Saviour. And he progressively saves us from our sins as we continue hiding in him, in short we actually become better people.

Our sources of strength

Be thou exalted, Lord, in thine own strength:
So will we sing, and praise thy power.

Psalm 21.13 (BCP)

God is our strength

Isaiah 12.2 (RSV) Behold, God is my salvation; I will trust, and not be afraid: for the Lord is my strength and my song, and he has become my salvation

The first Easter Day was all so unexpected. No one had reckoned with events on this scale. The likelihood was a bunch of dispirited, even disillusioned men, whipping themselves back to labour in which they had no more heart. They could not rid their minds' eyes of that recent sight of their dead Christ. Was it for this that they had left all and followed him? And the likelihood was a pathetic little group of women, for weeks on end, if not months and years on end, paying painful visits to a grave where all their deepest love lay ruined behind a large circular stone. The heart knows its own sorrow.

They had not learnt, and maybe we have not learnt, that what is probable or improbable in life as we know it is a wholly inappropriate measure for estimating how events will be wherever God is concerned. He may stand things on their heads. He has stood things on their heads. There was the Incarnation. Whoever would have thought it? There is the story of the Virgin Birth. Who can believe it? There is the resurrection of the dead Christ from behind a large circular grave stone not even two or three strong young women saw a hope of shifting.

But God is the sovereign Lord, sovereign over life and death, sovereign over human destiny, sovereign over our salvation. What we need to grasp is that God has acted, and will act, *for us*, beyond whatever we could even imagine. The future is bright now, our future. God has become our salvation. We have a source of undreamed of strength. What more right reaction than to trust and not be afraid.

> Strong in the Lord of Hosts,
> And in his mightly power;
> Who in the strength of Jesus trusts
> Is more than conqueror.
>
> *(C Wesley)*

Doxology
> Now unto him that is able to do exceeding abundantly above all that we ask or think, according to the power that worketh in us, unto him be the glory in the Church and in Christ Jesus unto all generations for ever and ever. Amen
>
> *(Ephesians 3.20,21)*

EASTER MONDAY

Holidays

1 Timothy 6.17 God, who giveth us richly all things to enjoy;

When we have completed some laborious task, expending our strength, we take a rest. We do this in order to recover our strength. The relaxation makes for recuperation and for re-creation. Unremitting toil debilitates. So does unremitting relaxation. There is a proper rhythm for life consisting in work and rest, labour and holidays. This is the way of wholesomeness, this is the way of healthy living.

Holy Week, crowned by Easter Day, represents the culmination of a gigantic task wrought by the grace of God in Jesus Christ our Lord. It effected nothing less than the redemption of the world. So the day following, Easter Monday, properly becomes a holiday because it is a holy day. The Catholic Church has always seen the Festival Days and Saint Days in this way. They are times for letting go, times for rejoicing in what has been achieved.

So take today off, and if not today, some other day. Holidays are important. They restore balance. They supply perspective. Rules cannot be formulated as to the way in which holidays should be spent because tastes differ and needs differ, but holidays should always leave us stronger in body and spirit.

Was Timothy, to whom two letters in the New Testament are addressed, in danger of being a little too solemn in his Christian profession, a little too life denying, instead of life affirming? Possibly. Hence the reminder to him (in 1 Timothy 6.17) 'God who giveth us richly all things to enjoy'. The sunshine, the fresh green of Spring, the song of the birds, a good play, a funny story, the love of a man or woman, a bottle of wine on a feast day. Why not? Did the writer of this letter try gently to lead Timothy to this idea as well? Perhaps it is worthwhile looking up 1 Timothy 5.23, even though this Monday is, or should be, a holiday.

A thought for the day
> Praise the Lord, O my soul:
> and all that is within me praise his holy name.
> Praise the Lord, O my soul:
> and forget not all his benefits.
> *Psalm 103.1,2* (BCP)

TUESDAY

Strength through joy

Nehemiah 8.10 (NEB) 'Let there be no sadness, for joy in the Lord is your strength'.

It must have been an extraordinary sight. Ezra the scribe standing high up on a wooden platform where all could see him in the town square in front of Jerusalem's Water Gate. Flanked on either side by other leaders in the community he solemnly opened the law of Moses and began to read. From early morning till noon he read. And not only was the law read out loud but expounded so that they all could understand. The people wept as they listened. They knew how far they had drifted from the precepts it enjoined which made for their national salvation. But they were instructed to dry their eyes. The day was indeed a holy one, but it was a day for rejoicing, not crying. 'Let there be no sadness' – so the message rang out – 'for joy in the Lord is your strength'.

And this is always true. To be downcast is to be weak. To be joyful is to be buoyant and strong. These people standing before Jerusalem's Water Gate had something to be joyful about if only they would realize it. So have we. As we stand in imagination before the walls of that same city Jerusalem we can hear how our sins need not stand a a barrier between us and God; how our salvation does not rest upon the quicksands of our own moral performance in life; how our destiny beyond the grace is no longer a matter for dreadful foreboding. Jesus Christ, the Son of God, once crucified is now risen from the grave *for us*. We should hear the message as it is proclaimed to us on Easter Day from whatever platform. We should understand the meaning as it is expounded *and rejoice*. The rejoicing is important. It is always important. We become strong as Christians when we rejoice as Christians. 'Let there be no sadness, for joy in the Lord is your strength'.

Jubilate
> O be joyful in the Lord, all ye lands:
> serve the Lord with gladness,
> and come before his presence with a song.
> *Psalm 100.1* (BCP)

Strength through hope

Hebrew 6.19 (NEB) That hope we hold. It is like an anchor for our lives, an anchor safe and sure.

However sturdily a ship may be constructed, however powerful its engines, it is not safe unless it carries an anchor, an adequate anchor. This is because there is no guarantee that any vessel will not on its voyage encounter storms of such ferocity that safety for it will consist only in riding out the storms *at anchor*. Strength to resist destruction will depend *on the anchor*.

The writer of the letter to the Hebrews in the New Testament tells us that we Christians carry on anchor. It is hope. Hope gives strength to ride out the storms of life. Here is a woman in German occupied France during World War II whose husband has been deported by Gestapo agents. She has not heard from him for a year. She fears the worst. But a member of the French Resistance gives her hope that she will see her man again. It was plain for all the neighbours to see that that hope was keeping her alive. Without it she simply lacked the strength to survive.

Our hope is in the promises of God who cannot lie. He promises to be our shepherd, to feed us in the green pasture, to lead us beside the waters of comfort, to restore our soul. And even when we walk through the valley of the shadow of death we need fear no evil, for he is with us. Moreover goodness and mercy will follow us all the days of our life and we shall dwell in the house of the Lord for ever.

'That hope we hold' and it gives us strength. It is not vague or doubtful. On the contrary it is like an anchor safe and sure. Easter has made it a hundredfold more sure.

Prayer

> O Lord, support us all the day long of this troublous life, until the shades lengthen, and the evening comes, and the busy world is hushed, and the fever of life is over, and our work done. Then, Lord, in thy mercy, grant us safe lodging, a holy rest, and peace at the last; through Jesus Christ our Lord.
>
> *(After J H Newman)*

THURSDAY

Strength through fellowship

Hebrews 10.24,25 (NEB)

> We ought to see how each of us may best arouse others in love and active goodness, not staying away from our meetings, as some do, but rather encouraging one another, all the more because you see the Day drawing near.

The Church to which this letter called 'Hebrews' in

the New Testament was addressed had grown sluggish and weak. True its members had faced difficulties and opposition but not in anything like sufficient ferocity to account for their debilitated condition. Various reasons are hinted at in the letter, and one of them was an evident slackness over the Christian fellowship. Bluntly speaking – some were staying away from the meetings.

From the days of its first life at Pentecost the Church was conspicuous for the vigour and tenacity of its fellowship. We read how the members met constantly to hear the apostles teach, and to share the common life, to break bread and to pray (Acts 2.42). It is not possible to remain a strong Christian, strong not only in conviction but in active goodness unless close touch is kept with the Christian fellowship. To grow slack in this matter is to become like a straggler in a column of soldiers marching through hostile territory. Safety lies in keeping up with the body of troops. Danger of being 'picked off' by the enemy is a probability for anyone who lets himself become isolated.

The Christian fellowship is grounded in the Risen Christ. This is its strength of cohesion. This is its latent power. There is a spirit present, not conspicuous in the world, the spirit of Jesus. We are unlikely to continue to breathe that spirit if we break our connexion with the fellowship, however ordinary it may at times appear to be.

Prayer

> Lord, keep me faithful to your Church
>   lest I lose my strength,
>   my strength of faith,
>   by which I live.

FRIDAY

Strength through weakness

2 Corinthians 12.9 (NEB) Power comes to its full
                          strength in weakness

This sounds pretty odd. 'Power comes to its full
strength in weakness'. The opposite might have been
expected – Power makes a feeble show in weakness.
But what is in mind here is not our power, but God's
power. And God's power does not compete with
ours. If we reckon that we are self-sufficient, that our
resources are quite adequate to cope with life, then
the power we have is all that will be available. God's
power will not operate in us.

Suppose, on the contrary, we reckon we are *not quite*
adequate for the demands life makes upon us, and
we seek God's power. Then indeed we shall know
something in experience of God's sustaining
strength. Perhaps this kind of halfway house is
where most of us who profess to be Christians live.

Suppose however when we are brought to the end of
ourselves, when we do not know which way to turn,

when every road ahead seems blocked, and we reckon 'the game is up', suppose then empty-handed we seek God's presence with no suggestion of our own to make, then it is that 'power comes to its full strength in weakness'.

This apparently paradoxical principle is spelled out to some extent in the context from which the verse is taken. St Paul had to endure a crippling disability but he was not crippled in achievement. On the contrary it threw him the more on to the divine resources of strength instead of his own, and out of that strength in his weakness, marvels of work were accomplished. 'When I am weak', he said, 'then I am strong'. (2 Corinthians 12.10).

Prayer
> Lord, take away from me the pride of self-sufficiency
>> lest I fail in my own weakness;
>> and when I have come to the end of myself
>> let me know in experience
>> the full resources of your strength.

SATURDAY

Strength in glory

Revelation 7.9–12,16,17 (AV)
> After this I beheld, and lo, a great multitude, which no men could number, of all nations and kindreds, and

peoples, and tongues, stood before the throne and before the Lamb, clothed with white robes, and palms in their hands; and cried with a loud voice, saying, Salvation to our God, which sitteth upon the Throne and unto the Lamb. . . . They shall hunger no more, neither thirst any more, neither shall the Sun light on them, nor any heat. For the Lamb, which is in the midst of the throne, shall feed them, and shall lead them unto living fountains of waters: and God shall wipe away all tears from their eyes.

Can we believe it? Can we believe that something like this is to be our human destiny? We began these Lenten meditations conscious of how life so often seems like a pointless merry-go-round with very little 'merry' in it. We go to work to earn money to buy the food to make us strong to go to work to earn . . . It does not continue like this for ever. One day the merry-go-round stops, and we fall off, as others before us have fallen off. What happens then? Does all our strength, all our spiritual strength, end in a hole in the ground or behind the curtain at the crematorium?

This is too hard to believe. Men and women since the dawn of human life have found it hard to believe. They have found themselves believing that life leads somewhere, though the 'somewhere' has been painfully indistinct.

Then into this obscurity there beams the light of Christ's resurrection. In him we too shall rise. So the whole prospect is wholly transfigured. Not only beyond the grave but on this side of it life takes on meaning and purpose. We are destined for eternity with God, eternity without pain, eternity without weakness, eternity without tears, eternity without human partings.

Not infrequently the bereaved enquire, 'Shall we recognize our loved ones on the other side?'. But what makes life worthwhile in the here and now? Is it possessions, or is it people? Life as we know it now is half dead without loving relationships. Love makes life. So then the life that is to be, life beyond the grave, life that is life in its fullness must be full of loving relationships. And God will wipe away all tears from our eyes.

Prayer

> Lord, strengthen my faith
> in the glory that shall be
> when your whole Church shall be strong
> and I, and those I love, glorying in the glory.

SUMMARY FOR THE WEEK

The Bread of life

No one is able to be strong who neglects bodily nourishment. In the modern world we are sharply conscious of this which is why we pay such attention to our intake of calories. Sufficient food and a balanced diet are essential for strength. For athletes they are a priority.

The same principle applies in the realm of the spirit. Spiritual nourishment there must be if there is to be spiritual strength. As it happens the world has been so ordered – divinely ordered we believe – so that even nature makes elementary provision for this. Most of us know what it means to drink in the wonder of some glorious landscape. We are in fact nourished spiritually by beauty. Music also fulfils this function. And is it all that uncommon to hear people say who have been cut off temporarily from their normal mode of living 'I feel absolutely *starved* for some music'? Art, literature, poetry – they all perform a function of providing nourishment for the human spirit which 'cannot live by bread alone'.

Over and above these categories of physical and spiritual nourishment the Christian, if he is to be a strong Christian, possibly if he is to survive at all as a Christian, needs a distinctive food. He needs the word of God. He needs to hear what God has to say, to feed on it, to take it into his system. Over and over again in the Bible there occurs this metaphor of feeding. The shepherd feeds his sheep, and God is a shepherd. Christ is called the Good Shepherd guiding his flock to suitable pastures. And with a transposition of thought Christ is the one *on whom* believers are called to feed. He is the bread of life, the water of life. In the Church we eat and drink sacramentally nourishing our souls into eternal life.

The word of God as food for the spirit we must have. The word of God as contained in the Bible must be ministered by the Church. It must be read in public worship so that it can be intelligently heard. It must be expounded and it must be applied. Without this nourishment the Church cannot be strong, neither can the individual Christian.

Our development from strength to strength is conditioned by how wisely and how well we are fed. God grant that the Church may be supplied with faithful and competent shepherds (the other word for which is pastors) ministering the Word of God, the Bread of Life.

Questions on the Weekly Themes

1. *Salvation in practice*
   - (a) What arguments are there for suggesting that our lives have no purpose except to go round and round? What against?
   - (b) Is our salvation a gift or an acquisition?
   - (c) In what ways is our salvation at risk today?
   - (d) Does a community need salvation? From what? For what?

2. *Recognizing grace*
   - (a) What do we mean by saying God is personal?
   - (b) Why is Christianity called a religion of grace?
   - (c) Can you give some examples of the grace of God in your own life?
   - (d) If Christians ought to be gracious as God is gracious what would this mean in practice?

3. *Exercising faith*
   - (a) How would you define a reasonable faith?
   - (b) Why can faith be described as a response?
   - (c) When is faith superstitious?
   - (d) What is meant by 'the faith'?

4. *A willingness for obedience*
   - (a) We think of obedience in connexion with law. Is it possible to be obedient to love?
   - (b) What is meant by disobeying the gospel?
   - (c) How could Jesus be obedient for us?
   - (d) Can you name some areas of conduct in which Christians may be expected to show their obedience to Christ?

5. *Christian life-style*
   (a) How would you describe the life-style of Jesus?
   (b) Considering the immense variety of cultural background is a recognizable Christian life-style possible?
   (c) What is worldliness?
   (d) Must Christians be separatists?

6. *Trials and tribulations*
   (a) Is suffering a necessary part of life? If so why?
   (b) In what way is suffering uniquely portrayed in Christianity?
   (c) How would you answer a sufferer who asked 'What have I done to deserve this?
   (d) Can life be properly described as a school of suffering? If so, how?

7. *The Saviour*
   (a) Why was Jesus crucified?
   (b) How can the death of Jesus cleanse us?
   (c) What do we mean by the phrase 'sacraments of the gospel'?
   (d) Why has the view been put forward that Jesus did not actually die on the cross?

8. *Our sources of strength*
   (a) When is the Church strong? When weak?
   (b) Do you think Jesus was a strong man?
   (c) What makes for a strong faith?
   (d) Can you name some strong characters in the Bible? and some weak ones?